Afterimages

Afterimages

A Family Memoir

CAROL ASCHER

HM

Holmes & Meier

TEANECK, NJ

Published in the United States of America 2008
by Holmes & Meier Publishers, Inc.
PO Box 943 • Teaneck, NJ 07666
www.holmesandmeier.com

This book has been printed on acid-free paper.

∞

Design and typesetting by Rachel Reiss

LIBRARY OF CONGRESS CATALOGING-IN-PUBLICATION DATA

Ascher, Carol, 1941–
Afterimages : a family memoir / by Carol Ascher.
p. cm.
Includes bibliographical references.
ISBN 978-0-8419-1449-0 (hardcover : alk. paper)—
ISBN 978-0-8419-1451-3 (pbk. : alk. paper)
1. Ascher, Carol, 1941- 2. Jews—United States—Biography. 3. Children of
psychotherapists—United States—Biography. 4. Children of immigrants—United
States—Biography. 5. Jews—Austria—Vienna—Social conditions—20th century.
6. Fathers and daughters. I. Title.
E184.37.A83A3 2008
973'.04924—dc22
[B]
2007046937

Manufactured in the United States of America

12 11 10 09 08   1 2 3 4 5 6 7 8 9 10

To those whose lives were overturned or
cruelly ended by the Nazi regime

And to their heirs, whose obsession
has been to find meaning in this history

Contents

Family Tree

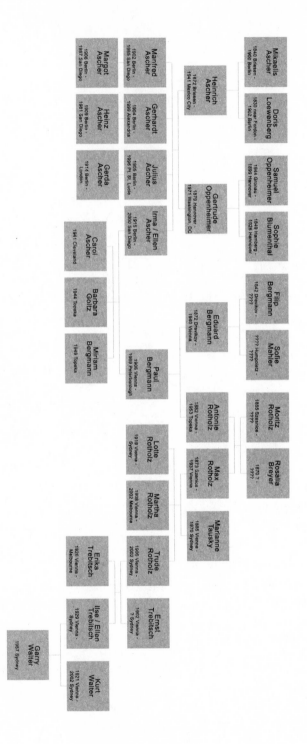

- Mikaelis Ascher — 1840 Bielen - 1900 Berlin
- Doris Loewenberg — 1835 near Fordon - 1912 Berlin
- Heinrich Ascher — 1872 Briesen - 1941 Mexico City
- Samuel Oppenheimer — 1844 Gnesta - 1899 Hannover
- Sofie Blumenthal — 1849 Hamberg - 1926 Hannover
- Gertrude Oppenheimer — 1879 Hannover - 1971 Washington, DC
- Manfred Ascher — 1902 Berlin - 1985 San Diego
- Gerhardt Ascher — 1904 Berlin - 1999 Pt. St. Lucia
- Margot Ascher — 1906 Berlin - 1987 San Diego
- Heinz Ascher — 1909 Berlin - 1981 San Diego
- Gerda Ascher — 1914 Berlin - London
- Julius Ascher — 1905 Berlin - 1969 Pt. St. Lucia
- Irma / Ellen Ascher — 1915 Berlin - 2000 San Diego
- Carol Ascher — 1941 Cleveland
- Barbara Goltz — 1944 Topeka
- Miriam Bergmann — 1949 Topeka
- Filip Bergmann — 1842 Dreykov - ????
- Sofie Mahler — ???? Humpoletz - ????
- Eduard Bergmann — 1872 Dreykov - 1940 Vienna
- Moritz Rotholz — 1855 Szasnice - ????
- Rosalia Breyer — 1870 ? - ????
- Paul Bergmann — 1905 Vienna - 1960 Peterborough
- Antonie Rotholz — 1882 Vienna - 1963 Topeka
- Max Rotholz — 1873 Szanice - 1937 Vienna
- Marianne Tausky — 1885 Vienna - 1970 Sydney
- Lotte Rotholz — 1919 Vienna - Sydney
- Martha Rotholz — 1908 Vienna - 2002 Melbourne
- Trude Rotholz — 1906 Vienna - 2002 Sydney
- Ernst Trebitsch — 1902 Vienna - ? Sydney
- Erika Trebitsch — 1926 Vienna - Melbourne
- Ilse / Ellen Trebitsch — 1929 Vienna - Sydney
- Kurt Walter — 1921 Vienna - 2002 Sydney
- Gerry Walter — 1957 Sydney

Only family members in my direct line, or mentioned in the narrative, are listed on this tree. For example, my Grandmother Gertrude had six brothers and sisters, none of whom are in the above tree, and my Grandmother Antonie had six brothers, of whom only Max is mentioned, since his wife and grown children emigrated to Australia and I recently reconnected with this part of the family.

Preface

In January 1939, Paul Bergmann, a Viennese *Gymnasium* teacher with psychoanalytic training had recently escaped his German-occupied country when he met a pretty, young, high-spirited Berliner, Irma Ascher, in a camp for refugee children not far from London. My father had only a transit visa for England, and was on his way to Hawaii, where he had been given a permanent visa; my mother would follow in six months. I was born in 1941, an uncertain mix of a moody Austrian intellectual, Jewish by heritage but secular and socialist in commitments, and a vivacious German woman, from a conventionally observant Jewish family, who had found Hitler's racialized curriculum too distasteful to complete her *Gymnasium* (high school) studies, but who had little natural interest in the questions of politics and religion stirring the left and the right. Without the rise of Hitler, the two would never have met or thought they were suited to each other.

My father was an immensely private man, who said little about his past. In a family of women, his silence contributed to the mystification of his maleness and created a force field of alarm between us and the countries from which he and my mother had fled. Though my father understood well the complicated history that had led to the exile or death of millions of Central European Jews, it was my mother, a storyteller and conjurer of romance, who gave us the simple family narratives that for many years formed our sense of our refugee heritage.

Afterimages represents an odyssey that started in the mid-1990s, when I began to reflect on the peculiarity of my childhood, growing up amidst a community of European Jewish psychoanalysts in the Midwest. As projects have a way of leading along unforeseen paths, I soon felt the need to understand my father's first thirty-three years in Vienna, about which he had said so little. A grant from the Memorial Foundation for Jewish Culture enabled me to spend time working in a range of Viennese archives in Fall 1995, and this visit was followed by a second trip a year later, in which I confirmed, corrected and added to my research. Thus, in Part I, I describe growing up and older in the shadow of the Holocaust, and, in Part II, I report on my long 1995 stay in Vienna, along with my discoveries about myself and my father. However, I am an unruly user of chronology, experiencing daily Freud's understanding that in our unconscious we live in an eternal present, where our experiences from different time periods bleed into each other. My method throughout the book has been to follow my own thoughts, with my childhood and my parents' childhoods playing counterpoint to what I have learned and who I have become.

The odyssey that has turned into this book has also been formed by circumstances outside the confines of the evolving manuscript. Trained as an anthropologist, until Spring 2007 I spent weekdays directing studies of urban public schools—which meant that much of the time I was inside a school, alone or with a colleague, interviewing and watching and taking notes. Thus, writing and rewriting this memoir was confined to the periphery: to early mornings before work; weekends, when I didn't have reports to complete; and all my vacations. Moreover, my memories and imagination, as much as the facts about my father and his family and the more general history I uncovered, were often painful and difficult to assimilate. I wrote narratives that I discarded or dramatically changed; reshaped themes that I eventually realized I didn't believe in, and so dropped; and drafted chapters that I then turned into articles or dumped into an ever-growing outtakes file.

In short, it was several years before a manuscript that seemed to encompass this odyssey was ready to share.

Many books, even the most successful by literary or financial standards, have prepublication stories of misunderstandings and rejections by agents and publishers. This book is no different. I was lucky to find Deirdre Mullane at the Joseph Spieler Literary Agency, a lover of books, a careful and intelligent reader, and an indefatigable agent, who placed my book. Unfortunately, the publishing company suffered a setback, and after several publication delays my contract was returned. There followed a second search for a publisher, and my manuscript finally landed safely at Holmes & Meier, where the publisher, Miriam Holmes, and my editor, Richard Koffler, have combined enthusiasm for the manuscript with due diligence regarding narrative details small and large. Needless to say, I take full responsibility for the errors that remain in the manuscript.

Several changes occurred in my life since I completed the manuscript. First, in Fall 2000 my mother died in California, having been a widow for thirty-five years. Second, I describe my youngest sister Miriam as psychologically fragile, even mentally disturbed. This was how she was when I was writing. Indeed, I would have predicted that she would be likely to go in and out of breakdowns for the rest of her life. But shortly before my mother's death, a brain surgeon who by chance observed her in a clinic waiting room diagnosed her as hydrocephalic. After many suspicious questions on our side, he performed an operation that inserted a shunt, relieving pressure on her brain. Another book could be written about Miriam's astonishing changes over the past years, only some of which can be directly attributed to the shunt. Suffice it to say, she has built a new life, which includes a circle of friends and a responsible part-time job, unimaginable at the time I was writing the book.

Readers may find it confusing that I use the last name, Ascher, my mother's maiden name. When I married for the first time in 1964, I changed my last name from Bergman (the final "n" had been dropped when I was in elementary school) to my husband's name.

That marriage ended in 1969. Year after year, I would decide to return to Bergman, only to find myself paralyzed. Though my father
had died in 1965, he remained an overwhelming and constricting
presence, from which I struggled daily to free myself. However, I
had become extremely close to my mother's older brother, Gerhard
Ascher, and his wife, Edith. Through them, I experienced Jewish observances I had never learned at home, even as they offered me
lively intellectual engagement and accepting warmth. Finally, in
1979, when I was already living with Robert Pittenger, who would
become my second husband, I had a dream in which I was reminded that Ascher was one of the early tribes of Israel. I decided to
take my uncle's name, which had also been my mother's.

Several chapters have been published in expanded or altered
forms in journals. The first chapter, "Prom Prelude" appeared as
"Dancing with Ludwig" in *American Voice*. "Der Rechte Weg" was published in *Confrontation*. More academic versions of the chapter,
"Force of Ideas", were published in *Lucifer Amor* and *Education History*. "My Father's Violin" appeared in *Shenandoah*, where it received
the Thomas H. Carter Prize in literary nonfiction. An early partial
manuscript of the memoir received an award from the New York
State Foundation for the Arts.

Finally, a number of people have sustained me while I researched
and wrote this book, as well as contributed to its content. My friendship with Thomas Aichhorn and Friedl Früh, whom I met in Vienna
in 1995, has been a rich addition to my life, and Thomas has been
generous with his grandfather August Aichhorn's papers, as well as
his own historical research. I had lost touch with the Rotholzes who
emigrated to Australia, but in 1996 the grandson of a cousin of my
father's, Garry Walter, got in touch with me by email. Through
Garry, I was able to question Lotte Rotholz, my father's cousin, and
Garry has also supplied me with memoirs by Lotte and other relatives 'down under.' My sisters, Barbara and Miriam, have been curious and generous observers of my process, eager to learn what I
was uncovering, and helpful with their own memories. My friend-

ship with Sara (Sally) Ruddick has been a source of lively, often hu-
morous conversation on subjects both critical to this memoir and
entirely unrelated; Sally also provided a final reading of the manuscript. Freddie Greenberg has been an attentive, deep and fearless
listener, whose ability to intuit my past and where I was headed, has
been a source of comfort, pleasure, hope, and unforeseen internal
release. Robert Pittenger, my loving helpmate for over thirty years,
has offered companionship and support throughout moody days,
long work hours, and repeated trips to Central Europe. Several
times, when my own curiosity or courage failed, he took it upon
himself to initiate the next step in my research and waited with gentle humor for me to catch up.

I

Growing Up in the Shadow of the Holocaust

1

Prom Prelude

I BEGIN MY STORY WHEN I WAS seventeen. It was 1958, and my family had recently moved to Bethesda, four miles from where General Dwight Eisenhower was in the White House. My father had worked at an experimental psychoanalytic sanitarium in Seattle until a heart attack sent him searching for more peaceful employment. Now he divided his time between studying modes of psychotherapy at the National Institute of Mental Health and seeing psychoanalytic patients in a downstairs office in our suburban home.

Our move from Seattle to Bethesda had brought me from a mediocre vocational high school to one of the very good high schools ringing the nation's capital. Behind the sprawling, neo-colonial high school a practice golf range wound along the sloped periphery of the vast football field. "Golf is the most important subject you'll take here," my young gym teacher informed me, as she hustled me along. Indolently, I swung my club, unable to imagine a future on the rolling green golf courses of the nearby country clubs whose gates I already knew were marked "restricted." Still, I felt I had entered a kind of paradise of serious academic subjects and disciplined well-dressed students, preparing for the Ivy League colleges and elite state universities.

Although the modern synagogue my school bus passed each day suggested that, for the first time, I had Jewish classmates, they were as invisible as I. In fact, since my parents observed no Jewish rituals, I was never even sure when the High Holidays came, and I couldn't have said which of my classmates' seats were empty. If there was another student whose parents had been run out of Europe, I never heard a hint of it. Just over a decade since the end of the Second World War, it seemed in bad taste to bring up prejudice and other Jewish concerns.

Among my new schoolmates were a few black students, but their courses were the vocational subjects I had left behind in Seattle. I felt an uncomfortable shame when I invaded their huddle on my shortcut through the school courtyard, in part because I knew I could "pass" for gentile, as they never could pass for white. Yet I also envied them the clarity of their genes and the comfort of their tight clan.

"Your father must be in the army," was the common response when I let slip that I'd been in Seattle only three years, and Topeka, Kansas was where I'd gone to elementary school. "Not really," I said with a grin, and tried to steer the conversation away from our family's peripatetic habits. Every new admission about my background only made me appear stranger. I could have agreed to be the daughter of an army or a navy man, but one of my parents' mandates was never to lie about who I was. Was silence a lie? I wasn't heroic, and I wasn't sure. Each time I toyed with omission, I felt the irritable melancholy of someone poking an infected tooth.

The truth is, I couldn't have pretended to be an army brat, for I had absorbed my parents' revulsion—more accurately, their fear—of anyone in military uniform. For years, the sight of a policeman had made my mother anxiously reach for my hand. I also knew that the sadism and brutality my parents had witnessed in Nazi Europe restrained them from even a quick slap to discipline me or my younger sisters, Barbara and Miriam. Stung by the cruel racial frenzy that had engulfed Europe, and staggering silently under their own losses as they tried to rebuild their lives, they believed that the only way to rise above their memories was to be rational in their dealings with us.

A master of theory and speculation, my father must have hoped that he could use his flights of the intellect to conquer his own violent temper. While he could charm anyone with his Austrian humor and courtesy, he was easily morose and harsh in his judgments, and a minor obstacle or irritation could be the last straw for him, evoking a sudden rage that thundered through our house.

What I recall is how my father gave a preoccupied shrug when I told him that I'd been invited to a weekend of double-dating at Annapolis, the naval academy two hours away. My new neighbor Marilyn, a flat-faced girl with a heart-shaped chin and pouting blood-red lips, had recently been crowned local beauty queen; she had a boyfriend at the academy, and needed someone to come along as a date for his buddy. My father had a deeply authoritarian side, but he was a pedagogical liberal, and he was convinced by the psychoanalytic discovery that repression backfires. If his daughter wanted to visit a navy man, he wasn't going to forbid her the experience.

The Annapolis weekend unfolded at an agonizing pace, with a stroll around town with our dates, a football game, a pizza dinner, a review of the naval fleet in the Chesapeake Bay, and a "semiformal" dance at the academy. Even Marilyn's happy chatter when we were briefly alone in our rented room wearied my patience, and I was relieved on Sunday evening to be safe at home, the agony suddenly worthwhile as I reported on the weekend to my father.

"We actually had to stand around watching the midshipmen salute the boats!" I told him. "They just stood at attention in their white uniforms, not moving a muscle, and that was supposed to be interesting. I was squirming, I was so bored."

My father smiled and closed his book against his finger. "I suppose it's good training for not giving into one's impulses, which is important when bullets are whizzing at you on a battlefield and you would like to run."

I nodded with contentment, letting my mind stretch and my experience expand with my father's insight, then offered him a new morsel to chew on. "The men changed into completely fresh uniforms before every event! They have two kinds of white, regular and dress."

"The cleaner the uniform the greater the capacity for brutality," he said dryly.

"You think so?"

He shrugged, as though unwilling to share what was crossing his mind. "I don't know, there's probably something in a uniform that, like standing at attention, prevents one from giving into individual fears and scruples—makes it easier to take orders, whatever they are."

My date had asked if I would come back, which had been both puzzling and flattering, I had shown so little of who I was. But now I reassured my father, "I'm never going there again!"

He nodded, pleased to have me home, and as he reopened his book I picked up the Sunday newspaper, eager not to push beyond the limits of his interest.

Although Marilyn and I both caught the school bus at the corner, I was gradually taking my distance. Instead, I saved a seat for a new friend, who climbed on a few stops after mine. Jocelyn was a tall girl with a turned-up nose and long slightly bleached hair that fell in careful waves. At different moments, I thought she looked stately and beautiful or vacuous, prim, a little silly; and perhaps her appearance did change from moment to moment, for she was an evanescent girl with a breezy, self-deprecating, whimsical style, who was as caught up in what was proper as she was obsessed with deeply ethical and spiritual dilemmas. (A year later, when we were seniors, in defiance of her family's high Protestant commitments, she fell in love with Catholicism and, anxious to become a nun, drove herself to a convent every Tuesday and Thursday after school for instruction with the sisters.)

Jocelyn lived in a beautiful colonial home, in a better neighborhood than ours. I had confided to her that I was Jewish, and I knew that after school she often stayed on the school bus until my stop for the adventure of spending a few hours amidst the vestiges of old Europe. She loved my father's leather-bound volumes of Freud and the German literary classics, and the special cakes with German names that my full-bodied mother would be pulling out of the oven, her thick brown hair curling from the kitchen's damp heat. Mother liked to pause before she cut the cakes, instructing Jocelyn in their pronunciation. *"Butterkuchen. Pflaumenkuchen. Sachertorte."* She made Jocelyn repeat the German word before she received a warm slice.

And Jocelyn waited for the heady discussions that my father prompted when he came out of his office between his analytic patients. "See here," he would say, pointing to an item about the Algerian War in the *Washington Post* on the coffee table. But his interest was less in whether France could win a battle in the Sahara than in why a European nation should continue to hold a country in North Africa. Wasn't Algeria, whose people spoke Arabic, not French, and were Muslim, not Catholic, across the Mediterranean from France? And was there a reason why any country should "own" another? This was what he wanted Jocelyn and me to discuss. "Oh, your family is so wonderful!" Jocelyn enthused. She dreamed of being like the King of Denmark, who was said to have worn the yellow Star of David on his coat to place himself at risk alongside his Danish Jews.

Romantic and rebellious, Jocelyn also liked to borrow her mother's Chrysler convertible and drive me to her parents' country club. My heart raced each time we sped past the "restricted" sign, our hair flying. We sat at a round white table on the poolside patio under a royal blue umbrella, she and I, eating club sand-

wiches held together by decorated toothpicks, and sipping our
Cokes, and I was as relieved (and guilty) to prove over and over that
my features didn't betray me to the waiters or other guests, as
Jocelyn was titillated by her defiant trespass. "You see, you really
could join this place," she said, picking at her sandwich. "Even your
last name—Bergman—could easily be Scandinavian. You even
look it. Really!"

"Jocelyn!" I stopped her, already confused by the latitude my
first and last names gave me, and vowing each time that I wouldn't
go back.

My father's unusual profession was something else I generally
kept to myself, afraid that it implicated me in a darker view of
human nature than was acceptable among my cheerful schoolmates and their optimistic families. ("Innocents," my father called
them, with distaste.) But for Jocelyn, the idea that my father might
glimpse the wild and dark desires of which she was unaware, was
yet another exotic reward for coming to my house. "Oh, I bet he
knows that I'm really a nasty witch," she said, her long arms flailing,
as she sank further in a chair in anticipation of his coming into the
room for a chat.

THOUGH I WAS doing well in school, with spring in the air my immediate hurdle was the junior prom. The excitement of the prom
was all around me. But what I felt was dread and foreboding. Attending the prom might not make me a successful all-American
teenager, but not being asked, which was all too likely, would cast
me among the social rejects, the unacceptable, the deficient, the
deviant and the abnormal. In fact, not attending was unthinkable—or rather, too easily imagined. It meant spending the
evening at home with my family, which was my deepest wish to
avoid. If I only knew how! I could predict that my mother, always
anxious to counter my sinking spirits, and inexperienced in such

American teenage hurdles, would suggest that my younger sisters and I sew or bake cookies, "spend a nice evening together," as she liked to say. But I couldn't bear the thought of succumbing to that. The problem was that, despite my meticulous observations of social maneuvering and etiquette, it was still mysterious to me how one got a date.

And so it came to be late April, with the pressure rising daily—especially since, with typical 1950s delicacy, the consensus in the girls' bathroom was that, after a certain day, it would be humiliating to accept an invitation. Jocelyn considered herself too tall for the high school boys. She was coming with a young man from the country club, a college sophomore whose age and mysterious academic occupation counteracted her inclination to scorn—almost, that is. She could work herself into a lather of high disdain that collapsed a few minutes later in excesses of self-mockery.

On the phone, we discussed what she should wear. Strapless formals were the vogue, but only girls who were "cheap" showed the curve of their flesh. I went along to a boutique on Wisconsin Avenue with Jocelyn and her mother, a leggy, well-groomed woman whose hair was arranged just like Jocelyn's. Standing on the pink wool carpet, surrounded by mirrors, Jocelyn giggled and poked mockingly at her body; her breasts were puny. Squeezing them, she tried to form cleavage. "Not like yours," she threw me a wide-eyed competitive look. Besides, her shoulders were ludicrously freckled! Meanwhile, her mother grabbed the back of a waistline appraisingly, as she told Jocelyn to hold still or stand up straight. Every motion of this American mother-daughter ritual engrossed me, even as it reminded me how much of an outsider I was, since, even if I could learn Jocelyn's part, my mother, who had never opened a copy of Vogue would have no idea of how to play her instructive and reassuring role.

As for my prom prospects, Jocelyn remained sure someone would ask me, but she couldn't say who. It was when she began to

run through names of boys at her country club whom she might
solicit in my behalf that I pretended not to care about the prom. "Really, Jocelyn, leave me alone! I'm not going out with any of them." To
my surprise, two girls in my French class—girls who had applied to
elite colleges for early admissions—also hadn't been asked. They
cracked cynical jokes about what I had assumed could only be a secret disgrace. Still, I was nowhere close to applying to college. I was
going to have to use summer school to make up the algebra and
trigonometry I had missed in Seattle.

Then one evening a male voice with a German accent was on
the other end of the telephone line. It was Ludwig, the school's
foreign exchange student from Hamburg. Ludwig was a tall,
sturdy boy with straight dark hair and pale skin and a few dark
hairs above his loose upper lip. Small eyes the color of black olives
were neither warm nor piercing. I didn't think I would have liked
his stubborn humorless looks had he been an American boy.
(Those few boys who turned my stomach inside out with lust,
whose eyes I was afraid of meeting, were the physics whizzes and
chess champions, themselves haunted by obscure preoccupations
and loneliness.) In any case, Ludwig was a German, and my parents avoided everything German, from Volkswagen cars to
Henckels knives (which they believed much sharper than any
American brand). Even the fact that Ludwig was spending the
year with our class vice-president, Tom, couldn't change his na-
tionality. Although Ludwig had learned English quite well during
his year in Bethesda, his every word reminded me of his origins.
With dread, I waited as he laboriously got out that he wished me
to accompany him to the prom.

When I hung up, my relief at finally being asked was blanketed
by bitterness. Ludwig!—why Ludwig? Oh God, why Ludwig? The
answer was clear. Ludwig and I shared a class, where I had let it be
known whenever he stumbled with his English, using the German
word instead, that I knew what he wanted to say. It was likely that
my willingness to come to his aid had made him think that I

would react kindly if he called. Why had I ever let out that I understood German?

Even so, I had a date! I was going to the prom. And since Ludwig was staying with Tom, I would be traveling in a car with the class vice-president, an immense step up the social ladder.

My father, who was practicing a sonata between patients, lifted his fingers from the piano when he saw me get off the phone and draw near. I mentioned in an off-handed way that the boy who had invited me was an exchange student from Hamburg. I couldn't even say the word Germany aloud. Perhaps I was hoping that he would forbid me to go. Then I could have had my cake and eaten it too, by staying at home with the assurance that I'd been asked. Yet, as with my invitation to the naval academy, my father kept his distance, only nodding before he returned to his beloved music.

Telling my mother was easier, since her opinions didn't carry my father's moral weight, and I had long ago learned to disagree with her. Now she argued that, after all the negative stories I'd heard about Germany, it was good that I was getting to know a real German, and he getting to know me. And she mocked my squeamishness. "Carol, the boy is your age. He was a baby during the war, just like you! Whatever his parents did, he can't be responsible."

After scouring my closet and reluctantly agreeing that nothing was suitable, Mother went shopping with me—to the sale rack of Woodward & Lothrop, the local department store. The dress we bought was a dark green iridescent satin with purple flowers. A high neck in front swooped downward from the shoulders to form a low V in back, and there was a drop waist that drew subtle attention to my curves. Although apparently no one else in Bethesda had wanted the dress, and perhaps it really was a winter dress, which was why it had been severely marked down, I loved the dress. I was also sure that it was beautiful, no matter how many girls had passed it by.

Mother was now bubbling with enthusiasm: it seemed particularly nice that I was going with a German, turning my prom into an international event, something she could share. Yet as I carried home the big rectangular dress box, I had to ignore the boy for whom I had made my precious purchase, or else I felt mortified, sick.

Tense with anticipation, on prom evening I took a hot bath, as Jocelyn had said she was going to do. Although Barbara had precociously begun going out with boys, she was only in the eighth grade and had never been asked to a prom. Now she and Miriam came in to watch me as I pulled on my new sheer stockings, hooked them to my garter belt, and slipped the satin dress over my head.

As the clock struck eight, I heard Ludwig's knock and opened the front door. Beyond our front lawn, I could see Tom and his date in the car. Ludwig was wearing a rented tuxedo, and held a box with the corsage I was to wear. With his scrubbed face and slicked hair, I thought he looked menacing and pathetic. Still, I had to act as if everything was normal, and maybe it was. As Mother had argued while I tried to relax in the tub, it was about time to think of reconciliation with Germany, especially since, by comparison with Jews like her who had been lucky enough to leave before the outbreak of war, it was the ordinary Germans like Ludwig's family who had endured bombing and famine and every manner of suffering.

But I knew that my father was unprepared for such reconciliation with either Austria or Germany. As I introduced Ludwig to him, he raised himself slightly from the chair in greeting, but his eyes barely strayed from the page he was reading. My mother, though, was engaging Ludwig with excessive enthusiasm. I had seen this before: her lavish friendliness to anyone who spoke German. She seemed to relish a conversation in which the pain of the past could surface merely by speaking her native language. Yet I could feel her tension as she eagerly wished us "viel Vergnügung"—a pleasant time. She was probably hoping that Ludwig would stop to ask where she was from in Germany, or even why she had left. Perhaps, too, she imagined finding a way to suppress her own sorrow and longing for a country from which she was exiled, and embrace him in a surreptitious reunion with her homeland. But Ludwig was as afraid of being openly curious about her as he was about me, and the two of us walked to the car.

In the school gym blue and red lights threw everyone into shadow, and the colored streamers hanging from end to end were a dark tangle above our heads. Standing at the edge of the wooden gym floor, Ludwig squinted at my pink program, which had blank lines for the name of my date, the flower he'd given me (it was a gardenia), and what I'd worn. "These are questions you should answer?" he said awkwardly, as he fumbled for a pen. "You can, but it's not necessary." I answered, wanting the prom program to remain uncontaminated by the compromises I'd made to come.

There is a moment when a boy must signal verbally, or with his eyes or hand, that you are to move with him onto the dance floor. Ludwig had learned a lot of American expressions, but he didn't know, "Wanna dance?" And he must have sensed that asking me in German would be unacceptable. As he gave me an impassive nod, I followed him obediently, and then he rested his hand tactfully on my satin dress, avoiding my bare back, and my eyes focused beyond his dark tuxedo, on the folded bleachers.

Dance after dance, Ludwig and I rocked in stiff rhythm to songs I swooned over when I listened to them on my bedside radio. Even during the slow songs, we kept our distance, Ludwig and I, and my arm ached from the effort of lifting it to his shoulder. At times, I caught Jocelyn pulling at her strapless gown as she whirled around the floor with her very tall date from the country club. I would have loved to take her aside for a few minutes of girlish confiding, but my confused misery went far beyond my words to understand it.

As I think back now, as much as I longed for the evening to be over, I must have wanted even more to crash through the crust of silence that held me imprisoned. What a relief it would have been to tell him, *Ludwig, ich bin Jude.* Would he drop his arms, aghast, in loyalty to a

Nazi father? I knew that Germans had moved into the homes of Jews as soon as they fled or were taken to concentration camp. Ludwig's family might even be living in the house of my mother's cousin, who, after escaping Hamburg, had been picked up in Holland and transported to Auschwitz. Yet as much as I needed to see Ludwig as an evil representative of the Third Reich, the person I really condemned was me. Like the French women whose heads had been shaved because they dated German soldiers during the Occupation, I was a deserter, a collaborator—and not even to keep from starving or to save my life, but merely to reach some distorted goal of popularity.

Perhaps, I now think, Ludwig had surmised that I was Jewish, and asking me to the prom was his own wordless act of reparation. How brave!

With Holocaust stories having become a mainstream line of entertainment, it is hard to imagine in 1958 that the word meant a natural disaster. Those Jews who had found their way to the United States tried to go about reconstituting their lives quietly, without making a fuss. Yet parents pass onto their children the emotional conflicts they can't manage. Steeped in the stories my parents cautiously shared with each other and with other émigrés, what I felt was only fear, bewilderment, shame, a corked rage. All their fears and bitterness and admonitions were fulminating on the gymnasium floor as the blue and red lights blinked and threw their long shadows. Finally, when the hands on the gymnasium clock had inched their way past midnight, I heard the last dance announced and knew with relief that we could soon leave.

My father had left on the front door light. Tom and his date drowsily reached for each other in the front seat as Ludwig accompanied me to the front door. There was a moment when I froze at the prospect of Ludwig trying for a kiss, as I believed was his right at the end of an expensive evening. But he shook my hand, and I escaped into the house. Temporarily safe.

I had no way to know that in six years I would be married, and that a little over a year after that my father would die of a heart attack, having angrily refused to speak to me. And I couldn't imagine that the displacement and loss of my parents' refugee experience, as much as my father's bursts of fury, would haunt my adult life, until I finally decided to confront them.

The Bergman family in front of 615 Lindenwood. At six, I was happy to be leaning against my father.

2

Der Rechte Weg

WHEN I THINK OF MY childhood, I think of Topeka and the white clapboard two-story house with its three upstairs bedrooms and full front porch at 615 Lindenwood. It was in the living room by the stairs that I practiced the violin to my father's moody, vigilant piano accompaniment. And it was both in the blue bedroom that I shared with Barbara and, later, after my father's mother Antonie moved away a few blocks, in her room papered in pink with white lace stripes, that I listened to my mother's stories of her own childhood in Berlin. Despite the shock my parents must each have felt as apartment dwellers from European capitals transplanted into a small Midwestern town, it was this simple very American house that gave me my own first sense of roots.

Lindenwood was shaded by expansive old mulberry trees on both sides, and in summer the sidewalks were stained purple with fallen berries. The street sloped upward from Sixth Street, where my father caught the bus each morning for the Menninger Sanitarium, and where Barbara and I sat kicking our feet against the cement retaining wall until his bus finally arrived in the early evening. Then we walked back happily, one hanging on each arm, as we tried to tell him all the day's news we had been saving just for him.

Most of the homes on our block were small but well-kept, and the yards were neatly trimmed. Our house stood in the middle of the block on a raise of land above the sidewalk; my mother was often out planting exotic succulents in a rock garden she had created at the sides of the steps, an unusual approach for Kansas that was never as pretty as she hoped. On our left toward Sixth, a one-story white bungalow with a sloped red roof sat sideways to the street, as if to display the standoffishness of the Catholic family whose children went to parochial school and who only rarely played with us. On our right, beyond our side yard where some years Mother planted a vegetable garden, stood a two-story house that was a duplicate of ours, though the house had a neglected air that made it seem mysterious and larger and its often unmowed yard was vast: as often as I tried to peer through its lace curtains, I could glimpse little of the elusive couple who lived there with a frail white-haired mother.

But the blight of the block from a real estate point of view was a busy laundry across the shady street. Extending back from the corner of Sixth Street four or five lots, almost far enough to face our Catholic neighbors, it sent out hot moist vapors, and the sidewalk was usually covered with lint, as if sticky snow had just fallen. I could kick at the lint as I walked by, trace a path with my footprints, or scoop it up and feel its tacky gray softness between my fingers. Yet my pensiveness as I passed the huge laundry window was also the result of my mother's concern that the black women at the vast ironing machines had taken work that white people wouldn't accept. In the summer, when the window was open to give the black women a breeze, I sat on its ledge and watched them shout back and forth, their pomaded hair in kerchiefs and their faces glistening with sweat. Sometimes they called out to me. "What?" I asked, excited but unsettled by the chance to talk to the women our neighbors ignored."You on vacation?"" This time I heard. "Oh yes, my school let out last week." "Wha'd she say?" I watched them mouthing explanations to each other; but even if I repeated myself, the noise formed a barrier as real as race, making it useless to carry on a conversation.

Directly across from us was the gray shingle house whose low front porch was covered with a faded green awning; like a half-sunken boat, it was the house where Mrs. Marsh lived. My mother tried to invent diversions to keep me home, but as with the sordid novels that some years later I would devour with intoxication even when I wished I could put them down, I couldn't stay away. Mrs. Marsh was an angular woman with a narrow, bony face and eyebrows tweezed to a feathery line. When she released the tiny pin-curls she usually hid under a silk scarf, they became a brown billow of waves, and she had the tense glamour of a movie star. She was the first on our block to have a television set, and she spent her days crocheting tablecloths and doilies while she sipped Coca-Cola out of the bottle, something I had never seen before. She would offer me a Coke, a frowned-upon drink in my house, while we watched one soap opera after another in her dark living room, cut off from the rest of the world. Why she put up with me, a little girl of eight, nine or even ten, who was often unsure what the oblique melodramas were about, I don't know; but I felt that beneath our differences in age, we were soul mates in our isolation. At the same time, I was learning from her, as well as from television, what adulthood American-style could be like, something neither my father and mother, nor my parents' circle of refugee psychoanalysts, could teach me.

WHILE MY CHILDHOOD memories unfold for me on Lindenwood in Topeka, inside that Midwest locale sits my mother's early home on Nassauischestrasse in the Wilmersdorf district of Berlin. As in a theater whose floodlight leaves other areas of the stage in shade, my mother's stories left dark gaps in my geography, but the nostalgic scenes she created formed a territory in my imagination which my Kansas home could never equal.

"Just think!" she would say, as she sat at my bedside before I went to sleep, or on those days when earaches kept me under the covers. Five minutes earlier, her sharp gray eyes had roamed my room in search of a disorderly shelf or a sweater left lying about, but now her voice had the achy pleasure of longing, and her eyes softened as they came to rest on the luxurious second-floor apartment on Nassauischestrasse.

Facing her street was a winter garden filled with plants and large windows on three sides. Behind glass doors, so that the sun streamed in, was a *Musikzimmer* with a grand piano in one corner, while in the other corner, by the door to the *Herrenzimmer* where my grandfather smoked his cigar, squawked a parrot in a large cage. At the back of the house, along the corridor to the children's bedrooms, on contraptions suspended from the ceiling, hung the bicycles of the four Ascher boys, which could be lowered whenever they wanted to ride into the countryside. Gerhard used the bike most often, for he was cultivating the family's vegetables in a little kitchen garden in the Dahlem district several kilometers away.

Sunday afternoons, the seven children were dressed in identical sailor suits: Manfred, Gerhard, Heinz and Julius with little sailor caps,

The Aschers in 1916. Grandmother Gertrude holds my mother, Irmschen; Grandfather Heinrich holds Gerda; Heinz (r.); Margot (center); Gerhard, Manfred, Julius (left to right) stand in the rear.

and Margot, Gerda, and Irmschen or Little Irma, the baby, all with large ribbons in their hair. After they had been lined up for inspection, their proud father led them and the *Kindermädchen* past the linden trees of Nassauischestrasse and across Uhlandstrasse, to Kempinski's, Berlin's best *Konditorei* and restaurant. There, at the largest table, everyone including the nursemaid was allowed to choose a slice of cake, along with coffee or hot chocolate topped with whipped cream.

Mother's favorite was *Baumkuchen,* or tree cake. Made on a rotisserie, when you sliced it, there were tree rings, and it tasted so delicious! "Was it like pound cake?" I asked, staring at the backyard trees beyond my Lindenwood bedroom window, but I was also seeing a striated piece of cake set out on a white tablecloth in the wonderful Berlin restaurant. "No, not quite." My mind's eye switched to the packaged cakes on the rack at the corner grocery store across Sixth Street. "What about a jelly roll?" No, nothing available in Kansas could give me even an inkling of the design or taste of this marvelous cake.

One afternoon Mother tried to make *Baumkuchen* using a recipe from my Grandmother Antonie's Viennese cookbook. Pulling the pan from the oven as each layer dried, she carefully ladled another thin spoonful of moist dough on top. As the oven's warm sugary odor began to smell familiar to Mother, her excitement mounted. But when the cake finally had three or four inches of thin layers, it was dry and hard on the bottom; even the tree rings hadn't come out right. Without a special rotisserie, the miracle couldn't be transported. (Years later, when we were finally in Berlin together, Mother would buy me a cellophane-wrapped *Baumkuchen* at the KDW, the big department store on the Kurfürstendamm. But, if I was an erstwhile Proust, savoring the gentle flavor of this plain cake as I ruminated on the nostalgia she had passed on to me when I was a little girl, Mother refused to be sentimental: perhaps her taste buds had been ruined by so many years of sweet American desserts, but to her the cake was dry and bland, and not worth the money.)

Yes, food had been rationed in the years after the First World War, but what she recalled was Papa bringing home a single banana to slice off a small section for each child, or giving them each a taste of his soft-boiled egg at breakfast. And if their ration cards were used up at the end of the week—well, then he gathered the entire family and the *Kindermädchen* to go to dinner at Kempinski's.

I could tell that Grandpa Heinrich had doted on his family, and perhaps especially on his youngest daughter, Irmschen, my mother. Also that my mother's fun-loving Papa had been utterly different from my own moody father, though Mother cloaked them both in rapture, without apparent distinction. Whereas my father found can openers bewildering, and his expression grew distracted if a faucet sprang a leak or a light bulb needed changing, my Berlin grandfather had been an engineer who adored contraptions. During the First World War, he had shown his patriotism and ingenuity by manufacturing steel crampons that enabled military horses to travel on winter ice. After the war, revamping the factory, he became the first German manufacturer of an electric vacuum sweeper, Vivos, which he promoted as *der rechte Weg* (the Right Way), intending to convince Berlin housewives to give up their brooms and mops. He must have been successful, for the family prospered throughout the economically turbulent 1920s until the Nazi years. But for my mother, Heinrich Ascher's grasp of *der rechte Weg* extended beyond electric sweepers or even a good knack for business, for her Papa had understood that in all endeavors the right way was that of gentle pranks, good-humored jokes, and generosity.

Perhaps his children had tasted their bit of egg at the edge of his teaspoon, and he was now straightening his *Krawatte* or putting on his hat before the large mirror, catching their adoring eyes in the glass "What will you do at the factory today?" Irmschen and Gerda wanted to know. The little girls were wearing their starched dresses, and large bows held their straight hair away from their excited faces. While the *Kindermädchen* wagged a cautioning finger at their

An ad for Vivos, promoting it as Der rechte Weg. The text beneath the photo insert makes the point that the new "dust sucker" can be used on carpets and curtains.

interrupting his concentration, Papa turned and threw them a gallant kiss. "*Ach*," he explained. "Exactly the same as you. I'll play with my dolls."

MY MOTHER DURING our Topeka years is a robust athletic woman, and her clear forehead from which thick brown waves are combed back suggests determination and good cheer. Free of the glasses she will wear later, her grayish eyes can be pensive or restless, or excited by a prank she is about to play, and her long straight nose and resolute chin give her a classic profile. Uninterested in the fashions of her new country, she confidently sews our dresses to meet the standards of quality and taste she remembers from Berlin, and she calls the patent leather shoes the other children wear to parties "vulgar" or "cheap." Sometimes her insistent light-heartedness irritates me, as does her boundless enthusiasm for projects by which she hopes to ameliorate a neighbor's loneliness, or solve human callousness and cruelty. "Until everyone is safe from prejudice, we aren't safe," she says in her heavy accent, her eyes suddenly burning as she prepares to leave for a meeting of the local NAACP. But when she is smocking the front of a dress or mending our socks, or even about to tell a story, her eyes are cast downward and there is a pleasant peace in her strong face. Though she measures only two inches over five feet, and complains of being short, to me she seems large, even statuesque, built of some pliant yet terribly durable material.

One day I realized that she wore no wedding ring, as other mothers did. "Why not, Mother?" I hated it when she was different from American mothers. She looked down at her sturdy well-shaped fingers, surprised either that they were bare or that married women were supposed to wear rings. Smiling, she began her story about the dime-store ring she and my father had quickly bought in England, after the judge had refused to marry even penniless refugees without a gold band. When their cheap imitation turned blue on her finger, she had tossed it out. Anyway, didn't having children make it clear she was married? "I guess whoever is confused can ask," she shrugged, uninterested in the romantic complications I was discovering on Mrs. Marsh's television screen across the street.

Though the *Deutschland* of Mother's youth has itself been transformed by the long shadows of the Third Reich, and her Berlin was divided by high concrete walls for four long decades, I find myself speculating on the energetic, middle-class German woman she might have become without Hitler—Jewish by genetic and cultural heritage, mildly observant, at home in a Germany still filled with Jews. She would have been a proper responsible citizen, urbane, with an edge of adventurousness. Although she was too young to understand the violent social struggles that shook Berlin during the 1920s, her older siblings passed on their excitement at the artistic and cultural freedom of the Weimar years: the theater of Brecht, the functional design of the Bauhaus. Like many German teenagers (including Nazis), she grew up a nature-lover, a hiker, and a gymnast; after school, she swam and practiced running, long jumps, javelin, and discus-throwing at the Sportsklub in the Berliner Stadium. (I would see that stadium for the first time as a young adult in Leni Riefenstahl's film, *Olympiade.* Among the scenes left out of this celebration of the 1936 Olympics were the many *Juden unerwünscht* (Jews not wanted) signs that had sprung up along the streets of Berlin and were temporarily taken down for the international visitors.) Like many Germans and German Jews, though not Nazis, she also looked forward to the victory of reason over irrationality and superstition—an optimism she held to the end of her life. This is why I find it hard to isolate how leaving everything behind and starting again in a new country changed her.

Here, in America, she saw herself as forward-looking and sensible. She was as scornful of anything she called old-fashioned as she was of émigrés who held onto the traditions of their former countries. "You have to look forward, you can't look back," was her mantra, recited with equanimity or determination or, more rarely, wistfulness. Unlike my father, whose attention was caught by the dark undertows and minor keys, Mother liked flat surfaces and the bold cheer of primary colors. Even my father's profession of psychoanalysis turned upbeat and uncomplicated in her rendition. "Spill it out!" she advised, as if talking about mental anguish, like pouring out milk that had gone bad, simply disposed of the anguish. Memories, for her, could be held onto or given away as simply as the clothing that she made us sort through each season to make sure we kept only what could be hemmed or let out to fit. Though her English was faulty, she called German "Hitler's language" and increasingly avoided speaking it. (Years later, when she visited me in New York, I thought to please her by taking her to the German Jewish community in Washington Heights, but she was revolted to discover that in America Jews still walked the streets speaking German to each other, "as if they never left home.")

Where in the living rooms of other families on Lindenwood one sank into soft upholstered chairs and couches, Mother covered rattan and wood garden furniture with hand-made canvas cushions in brown and green, the colors she attributed to nature. Instead of dark shiny wood cabinets filled with dishes, figurines and personal keepsakes, we had bookcases built of pine planks held up by glass bricks. Our light and sparsely furnished living room was decorated with several modern paintings, the most conspicuous of which was an enormous cubist-style portrait of an elongated and sorrowful black man with large oval eyes and blue and mahogany skin. If my father identified with the man's lonely grief, for my mother the painting affirmed for anyone who came into our house her alliance with those who suffered from bigotry, including in her adopted land.

Still, our household was graced with several mementos of old Europe. There was the sterling silverware, part of the large, ornate, monogrammed *fleischig* set my mother's parents had somehow hidden from the Nazis when they came to collect silver for the Third Reich. The set was now divided among the three sisters: Margot had eight place settings in Chicago, Gerda was storing her pieces in her home in London, and we had our settings for eight. Mother would tell me to be careful of the knives, whose handles came loose if left soaking in hot dishwater; but we used the heavy silverware everyday, even when we ate outside in the backyard. There were also the leather-bound volumes of Goethe, Schiller, Lessing, and Heine; a complete twelve-volume set of Freud; and an old German Bible with an Old and New Testament, which my atheist father had for mysterious reasons carried out of Vienna and now took with us from move to move, explaining only that it was also literature. And there were the small carpets my Grandmother Antonie had brought out of Vienna. Though I loved their density of pattern in rich melancholy shades, and the aura they gave of an Old World intricacy, Mother viewed them with the general impatience she felt toward her Viennese mother-in-law; they interfered with her vacuuming, and she eagerly let my grandmother take them with her when she finally moved out.

IN THE 1940S, my father's mother was a tall, straight-backed woman whose breasts lay flattened under dresses in the subdued colors of mourning. Her eyes were sharp behind her glasses, and a gold front tooth gave a disconcerting gleam when she spoke.

Her gray hair was a daily problem for her to comb. "*Ach! Es tut mir Weh,*" she winced, as she carefully pulled her comb through it. I stood next to her, my reflection as high as her shoulders in the full-length mirror on her closet door. In Vienna, the *Friseurdame* had come to her house every Friday before the Sabbath to wash her hair. In Topeka, she translated her weekly ritual into a Friday trip across Sixth Street to the beauty parlor behind the filling station. Sometimes Barbara and I sat on either side of her as her head disappeared inside the heavy metal beehive, and like conspirators we three browsed through the comics and confessionals that Mother called "*Dreck!*" and wouldn't allow in the house.

When my grandmother's hair was dry enough to comb out, it stood as stiff as tiny metal pipes that showed how pink her head had

Antonie Bergmann holding Barbara, while I sit at her side, suggests a stronger and more resilient woman than the grandmother who irritated my parents.

become from the heat. The next day, the wave was already losing its shape; and by the end of the week, her hair lay matted and lifeless, her scalp pale and flaking, because she found it so difficult to comb.

Grandmother Antonie had a friend, Mr. Eckstein, the widowed father of another Viennese psychoanalyst at Menninger, with whom she played Tarok, a middle-European card game. Mr. Eckstein senior was a stocky man whose solid belly forced him to lean back in his chair. As his thick darkly tanned fingers worked his cigar, a big gold ring flashed in the light.

"Ja, was noch?"—*"Siehst?"* Mr. Eckstein and my grandmother spoke loudly in their Viennese dialects, as they sat at the folding table

Mother had brought onto the front porch. *"Das ist eine Zehn,"* my grandmother announced, slapping the ten of hearts onto the table. Mr. Eckstein's cigar moved from the side of his mouth to the edge of the glass ashtray where he tapped out little ash patties. *"Ja, aber ich hab' einen König. "* Looking unconcerned, he displayed his king. The whole porch took on a rancid smell; and my mother, who usually refused to be concerned about the opinions of neighbors, grew irritated that uneducated Austrian dialect and cheap cigar smells were wafting from our porch.

"You want the cigar band?" Mr. Eckstein would ask me, when I sat on the porch rail, watching them. "This band is a little prettier than last time, no?" I loved the paper rings, which tore even when I was being careful, and was always grateful for a replacement. Cautiously, I slipped the new black paper band, with its red print and gold trim, on my finger, then held out my hand for my grandmother to see. *"Ach, wunderschön!"* she said quickly, before returning to her cards. *"Was hab'n Sie nun getan?"* (What did you just do?) She didn't trust Mr. Eckstein and was afraid that he was about to pull some trick on her.

MY MATERNAL GRANDFATHER, Heinrich Ascher, had grown up on a farm near Briesen, a little village in West Prussia whose name changed to Wabrzezno when it became Polish territory after World War I. Always the aristocrat, my mother's mother, Grandmother Gertrude referred to her husband's origins by noting only that his train had arrived in Berlin "at the wrong *Bahnhof*"—that is, the eastern station. Although my mother adored her fun-loving father and modeled her own ebullience on him, it was her mother who gave her the pride of Jewish royalty, and her unwavering confidence, even here in a strange land, about what was correct in all matters of comportment and taste.

Gertrude Ascher had grown up in Hannover, where her father, Samuel Oppenheimer, owned the Hannover Bank. Although he was dead by the time she married Heinrich, the bank was being well run by her older brother, Otto, and she had brought a substantial dowry to her marriage.

Photographs of their early married years show my grandmother Gertrude as a stout but erect woman in Victorian clothes. Her thick hair is brushed into a large knot, and precious stones dangle on either side of her square unsmiling face. Heinrich, who loved the idea of a large family, is said to have bought her a piece of fine jewelry to commemorate the birth of each of her seven children. Since no amount of gold or precious stones could ease the wear of continual childbearing on her body (she would be bent like a shrimp in old age) or the burdens of managing an ever-growing family, the jewelry seems to have done little for her stern demeanor. It was she who carried the heavy ring of keys, locking every door and cabinet from the maids, and it was she who tried to place restraints on her husband's open-handed joviality.

I WAS ALMOST seven the summer of 1949 when we took a train to see my Grandmother Gertrude. She was living in a tiny apartment on Grande Boulevard in Detroit, where the thriving postwar auto industry was employing her son Gerhard, an engineer. Her husband Heinrich had died of malaria in Mexico, at the end of a long and arduous journey from Berlin. She had turned into a small frail woman with a thin gray knot at the top of her head and was beginning to show a hunched back. On her bed, she carefully displayed for me her pairs of elbow-length kid gloves in white, beige, chocolate brown, dove gray, and black; her large silk scarves in exquisite patterns; her jewelry case lined in moss green velvet; and the hairbrush and matching manicure set with their tortoise-shell handles. This was her remaining proof of the lady of consequence she had hoped to be as a girl in Hannover, and had almost become in Berlin.

Though my mother was often imperious with Grandmother Antonie, she was a little afraid of her own mother. Suddenly there was an extra lightness and urgency to her step, and something of the little girl, as she said, *"Mutti, setzt dich,"* Mummy, sit down, deferentially opening the special folding chair she had brought along to Belle Isle, so that Grandmother Gertrude wouldn't have to sit on a hard picnic bench. It makes me wonder how often my Grandpa Heinrich, who needed to satisfy and delight, must have tried to soften his wife's severity. I know that after she had lost a diamond earring on the beach in Heringsdorf one summer, Heinrich secretly had a duplicate made, but waited until the next summer when they sat on their deck chairs to stir up the sand and—*"Ach! Schau mal!"*

Did she smile then?

LIKE GRANDPA HEINRICH, Mother knew the joy of giving, but her instincts to reach out were generally limited to extending a helping hand. Other women rarely telephoned Mother to chat when I was a child, and I don't recall her going out for coffee or lunch with a friend. Nor did she and another woman ask each other for confidential advice or laugh uproariously over their troubles, as I and my friends do so often. "I don't have time to socialize," she said, quick to enumerate the tasks that lay ahead of her. Besides, she believed that as a happily married woman she needed no one but her husband.

Having turned her back on Germany, Mother was reinventing her life in the Midwest, and at the center of her adventure was the Austrian who had swept her off her feet in the English refugee camp. But unlike the TV dramas that enthralled me, her romance brooked neither betrayals nor misunderstandings. Instead, the flow of her days was shaped by my father's schedule, desires, and intellectual interests. Ten years his junior and much less educated, she looked up to him for his superior knowledge and wisdom, accepting his corrections and even his derision as just reminders of her secondary status. He was her *great love*, her father, teacher, older brother, mentor and guide; and their marriage, whose romantic beginnings had been heightened by dislocation and uncertainty, was the *perfect marriage*.

Yet my father was as treacherous an ally for her as he was for me and my sisters. Easily distant, wounded, morose, or irritable, and suddenly enraged, his kindness and affection and playful humor were evanescent, unpredictably turning into their opposites. He might come into the kitchen to lay an affectionate arm on Mother's shoulder as she stood preparing food, but five minutes later, when she came into the living room where he was reading to lay a kiss on his cheek, he would pull away or wince. Which is why I suspect her of elevating him to the realm of mythology. For she, who remembered growing up so loved by her father and older brothers and sisters, insisted that she had never imagined so beautiful and complete a love as that which she now had with her Paul.

Mother had inherited Gertrude Oppenheimer's sense of being above the crowd, someone who didn't lower herself to the pedestrian tastes and desires around her. "The caliber here is so low," Mother would say, echoing her husband's view of both American standards and the quality of their new neighbors. "Women want to look cute?" she would ask rhetorically, shocked that such an undignified concept would be taken as praise. She was incredulous that anyone would call their spouse "honey," as if penetrating sweetness was what one sought in a mate. "This is a country of conformists," she said derisively. Though each person I met at school or on my street looked unique to me, I could see how they paled beside my mother and her wonderfully exceptional husband, my father. Perhaps her contempt was the other side of a discomfort in being too different to join in. In Berlin, she had been proud to be indistinguishable from other Germans—while the Ascher family kept kosher at home, the women didn't cover their hair, and the family didn't make a fuss about combining milk and meat when eating in Berlin's best restaurants.

Mother was not alone in believing that America had a degraded "mass culture"—the phrase was not hers but that of the sociologists of the 1950s, German Jews who, with the shrewd eyes sharpened by trauma, were developing a critical analysis of their country of exile.

But her confidence about what was high quality, attractive, good manners, necessary decorum, and even appropriate to eat, suggested that she herself had come from a society in which people conformed to a narrow range of acceptability. Although that world of assimilated bourgeois Jews was geographically far away and virtually destroyed, her proud sense of individuality was in part the result of living on very different soil.

Perhaps all snobs purchase their superiority at the expense of their own comfort and security. My mother's curtailed education was a constant source of humiliation. Like Groucho Marx, that paragon of Jewish self-contempt, she didn't have the confidence to meet those she deemed worth getting to know. "They won't find me interesting," she said of my father's refugee psychoanalytic colleagues who came to visit, as if the only worthwhile qualities were those she lacked. When they played chamber music with him, she busied herself with what she knew best, making the European pastries she knew they longed for. She was a housewife who believed that caring for a husband and children was a proper and sufficient role for her, yet she was contemptuous of other women who stayed at home, without making what she thought of as a larger contribution. She might have read on her own, becoming self-educated, but the barrier of a new language seemed too formidable, and she was not inherently curious about the worlds books could reveal. Belatedly, when I was in the fifth grade, she took a high school equivalency exam and slowly, like a frightened animal, began to gnaw her way through courses at Topeka's Washburn College, one subject at a time. Yet she remained self-deprecating about her learning: although American teachers demanded so little, she still found the assignments difficult. She sat hunched at the makeshift desk she had installed under her bedroom window, a woman built for physical activity and the busy comforts of entertaining, and anyone passing the half-closed door saw her uneasiness and lonely distraction.

———————

A PHOTOGRAPH TAKEN in front of Nassauischestrasse 26 in 1933 shows the white stucco apartment building, with its wide second-story windows that brought light through the winter garden. Parked out front is the new white Nash convertible that Gerhard and Julius had just brought back as a trophy of their year as engineers in Detroit. My mother stands smiling in a print sleeveless dress with a round white collar, her elbow resting breezily on the car's open top. Decked out in a driving ascot and a jaunty beret, Julius sits behind the wheel, and blond Gerhard is in the back seat. Papa Heinrich is in the seat next to the curb, near my mother. A round balding man with a white goatee, he seems to have shrunk compared to his youthful sons, and though he smiles at the camera, there is nervousness in his eyes. Perhaps the look can be partly explained by the events of that year, for the Nazis have gained a bare majority in the Parliament, and Hitler has just been appointed Chancellor.

I construct the next period from bits and shards, for my mother talked very little about her last years in Germany. Where every childhood story was a romance with her cast as the beloved princess, when she spoke of the *Hitlerzeit*, her voice became wistful, pensive, and filled with hurt. Like a little girl who has been well-behaved and can't understand why she has been punished, she was besieged by a swirl of unexpressed emotions about the injustice of her fate.

Actually, she chose her memories of this time like someone picking the few edible grapes from a rotting sprig. I know that month by month her life became increasingly curtailed. The curriculum in her *Gymnasium* had been Nazified: whether the course was history or biology, the lesson was that Germans were the master race and Jews responsible for every degradation, pestilence and defeat. Some of her gentile friends had become ardent Nazis, and though Jewish students weren't yet officially banned from public school, when a school friend she had trusted crossed the street to avoid her, she found it too unpleasant to go. So it was somehow her fault, as she saw it, that she hadn't had the fortitude to complete her education.

She simply didn't have the stomach to go on. To learn something and occupy herself, she studied sewing (a skill that she would turn to good use by making most of our clothes). She could still take a walk, even if she wasn't allowed to sit on a park bench—but what was the joy in passing signs that read "Jews Not Wanted" or her friends and neighbors who were afraid to say hello? They had been forced to give up their Christian maid so she sometimes shopped for groceries, but even that could be unpleasant, as the shopkeepers suddenly declared themselves out of carrots or meat when a Jew walked into the store. When the law forbade Germans from buying from Jews, my grandfather installed the family in a simple apartment behind the Moabit factory whose vacuum sweepers were no longer in much demand. Then the factory itself was confiscated and an Aryan became its new owner. When the Gestapo took over the bottom floor of the building, the family risked an unpleasant encounter each time they went between the apartment and the street.

ONE DAY WHEN I was around ten, as Mother and I were out walking, the air became still as she seemed to struggle over whether to yield to a memory. They were living behind *der Rechte Weg* factory, she finally said, and since Gerda had left to join her brothers in Spain, she was the last of the seven Ascher children in the house. Papa Heinrich was dragged out of bed in the night and taken downstairs. All night long, they worried. When he returned in the morning, he was barely able to stand. After a few moments, I asked fearfully, "What did the Nazis do to him downstairs, Mom?" She shook her head. "Some kind of torture." "What kind?" Again, she shook her head, and I was ready to distract myself with some children playing nearby, when her voice seemed to moan like the wind.

"They did something terrible—with electrodes to his penis. Just for fun."

On Thursday, September 8, 1937, the day Mother turned twenty-one, Heinrich handed her a visa and a ticket to London. (He was sixty-one, and for the moment he and his wife would still try to hang on to their lives and dwindling possessions in Berlin.) There were no birthday presents, no cake, no guests to celebrate her new adulthood; instead, she spent the day packing the single suitcase with which she would leave Germany. An Orthodox cousin living in London, who had just lost her husband and needed help with her six children, had sent my mother a visa as a domestic worker.

Mother left at dawn the next day. Like all citizens of the Third Reich, she was allowed to take only ten marks out of the country, and she held these marks in a little bag tied under her blouse as the boat pulled away from Bremerhaven and her last sight of Germany for forty-two years. A few hours later, she arrived in England; it was now Friday afternoon. To reach her cousin's house before the Sabbath, Mother rushed across London by cab, spending every shilling into which she had converted her allotted ten marks.

IT IS 1979, and I am in Berlin with Mother, courtesy of the German *Wiedergutmachungsprogramm*. This reparations program offers a week in Berlin to Jews who were forced out of Germany, or lived in hiding, or survived the concentration camps of the Third Reich. Over and over, as we visit Kempinski's and the many other charmed places where Mother learned *der Rechte Weg*, she and I have the same conversation. We see a woman, man, or couple her age, and she sighs, "Na, I wonder what they suffered during the war."

"Maybe they were Nazis," I casually reply, struck by how much better dressed the Berliners are than we.

"Carol, you can't know what they did. And the war—the rations and the bombing—it was terrible for everyone. I was lucky to get out!"

"I think you're projecting, because you're unable to face your own suffering," I tell her, stubbornly continuing the battle we've waged since I went to the junior prom with Ludwig.

On a rainy morning, I orchestrate a drive past her father's factory in Moabit. She winces at the sight of the building where she spent her last months in Berlin, and quickly turns away, and a few minutes later she sighs again with relief at being among the fortunate, those able to leave while things were still relatively safe. Which, by now, I know has more than a strand of truth.

Toward the end of our visit, on a cold gloomy Sunday afternoon, we chance upon a flea market in the square across from the Charlottenberg Palace. The open market spills with old velvet curtains, silver teapots and candelabras from the turn of the century, damask tablecloths, and stray plates from expensive sets of china—"Like we used to have," Mother murmurs from time to time. Moving among the stalls, we touch a strip of lace, inspect a crystal vase. It might be a flea market in the United States, except that everything is heavy, dark, and ornate. Mother has discovered a silver egg-cup like the one from which her father gave his children tastes of rationed soft boiled egg. She wants to take it back to Miriam, but she can't get herself to buy it, and seems distressed.

"If you like, I'll buy it," I volunteer, opening my purse.

Tight-lipped and suddenly pale, she shakes her head, and a few minutes later, I steer her out of the market. When we have rounded the corner, she says quietly, as if coming upon the words to resolve her conflicted temptation, "It's not nice to buy a gift in a flea market." Yet I suspect that what she found unbearable was the prospect of buying back an egg-cup that just might have been her family's.

It is the evening of that Sunday when we see Beethoven's *Fidelio* at the Berlin Opera House. To find her husband, who is being starved in the Spanish prison's dungeon, Leonora disguises herself as a man (Fidelio) and becomes a prison guard, inadvertently winning the infatuation of the head warden's daughter. Tears stream down my face during the glorious last chorus, as Leonora/Fidelio, her husband, the other prisoners, and even the prison officials, all sing to the triumph of justice and a woman's courage.

"Think of how terrible to find you've been so fooled," Mother breaks into my grandeur of feeling. Suddenly I realize that she has been identifying with the naiveté of the prison warden's daughter.

And I am so moved by her inadvertent confession about her own lack of worldliness that, wiping my eyes, I put my arm around her shoulder, and I can only wonder what experience during our trip has made her fear having been fooled by her native city.

3

Dark and Light

MOTHER'S GENIUS WAS TO transform my Kansas childhood days with a sweetened past, the fanciful and the exotic. She noticed what we needed to turn a table or a few chairs into a fort or a secret castle, and she would lean over the sheets of grainy paper on which Barbara and I were attempting the likeness of wild animals with our crayons. "See here," she said as, dropping to her knees, she quickly sketched a monkey in shades of brown and green, his long arms outstretched as he swung between two tropical palms. The trees she recalled from Hawaii, her first home in the greater United States, though I'm not sure about the monkeys, and she could draw giraffes and kangaroos, which I'd seen through the bars of our cramped little Topeka zoo. But she gave her animals grass and trees and a wide blue sky overhead. When I wanted to save a drawing, though, or show it to my father, she became diffident. "It's just a sketch," she said, studying it critically. "I don't think I got the head right." And she plied her crayon a little more on the outline, somehow still keeping the style airy. "No, it's still not quite right."

Even serving us simple sandwiches on a bright Fiestaware plate at lunch gave Mother the discomfort of a task unembellished, incomplete. At the least excuse, she asked if she should make us each a

Struwwelpeter, the German prankster. Then Barbara and I sat kicking our heels against our wooden kitchen chairs until she brought us each a *Struwwelpeter*. His wild smiling face was a decorated hard boiled egg topped by flaming uncut hair of grated carrots; a tomato half had become his fat body; and, because *Struwwelpeter* refused to cut his dirty nails, his hands were carefully splayed slices of pickle. "Isn't that nice?" she asked, joining us in admiration of her handiwork. I nodded. But I was in a quandary: I hated to destroy my *Struwwelpeter*, and tried to interest Barbara in a serious discussion about the least offensive place to begin. Dirty nails? Hair? At least if I picked on a little grated carrot, my violation wouldn't be noticeable for awhile. But I could barely get myself to touch the orange hair. "I won't make you a *Struwwelpeter*, if you can't eat your lunch," Mother laughed. Although I knew it was silly to make such a fuss about destroying a fairy-tale boy, I had an exaggerated fear of hurting things—even breaking a cobweb made me uncertain. My father warned me that I was becoming too identified with suffering, which was true. My world seemed an inseparable tangle of what I could hurt and what could hurt me. I looked over at Barbara's plate: *Struwwelpeter's* head was gone, and my sister's full cheeks were working on the egg.

It was Mother who, when I was six, also invented our own private way to celebrate Christmas—a ritual in which we wouldn't be disloyal Jews. This was during the years when the winter holiday season went unmarked, before she sometimes ignored my father's sarcasms about religious observance, and lit the Chanukah candles.

On a cold December evening after dinner, the first in what would be our private tradition, Mother took Barbara and me to see Kansas Avenue, Topeka's main business street, aglow with Christmas lights. Snow had fallen, and we were bundled up with woolen caps, mittens, and galoshes. At the corner of Sixth Street and Kansas Avenue, we climbed down from the bus, and with Mother between us, we each took a hand. Walking slowly along the dark slushy sidewalk, we admired the red, white, and green lights in wreaths of pine needles looped around the telephone poles and strung across the street in thick slack braids. At every store window, we paused to gaze at the festive displays: the toys tied in red ribbons and the women's high-heeled shoes curling around poinsettias; the housewares dripping with tinsel; the elegant boxes of stationery draped with velvet and netting, and the fancy dresses meant for parties unlike any my mother was invited to. All the while, hidden loudspeakers issued a crackly: "Oh, come all ye faithful! Joyful and triumphant!"

As a first-grader in Miss Eddy's class, I had learned *"Silent Night"* and *"Joy to the World"* to prepare for our performance at the school Christmas pageant . (This was long before the Supreme Court acknowledged America's growing diversity by banning Christian prayer in public schools.) Even my father was happy to play Christmas carols on the piano. He had a German book of carols that contained, *"O Tannenbaum! O Tannenbaum! wie grün sind deine Blätter,"* and he encouraged us to sing along with him in either German or English. Religious music was still music for him, thus raised above both the hypocrisies of those who prayed piously but lied or cheated outside the church or synagogue, and the deeper problem of how to respond to a God who had turned His back while the Nazis exterminated Jews. But my sharp new awareness that all my classmates, as well as my teacher, celebrated Christmas—that the other houses on Lindenwood were decorated for the holiday as the world around me turned in an accelerating spiral of festivity—had made me come home from school a little forlorn. "Why can't we have a Christmas tree?" I asked Mother, shaking my arms out of my coat sleeves.

"Because we're Jewish."

Then did being Jewish simply mean doing without? "Do we get Christmas presents?" I already knew the answer.

"No, we don't celebrate Christmas—we don't believe in Christ."

Miss Eddy said that Jesus had been a real man, and a plaster baby Jesus was being installed in a manger under the enormous Christmas tree in the school's entrance hall. In a book of Sienese paintings from my Aunt Margot were beautiful images of a soft sorrowful

man with long, light brown hair—also awful images of him hanging on a cross. And in my father's book on psychosomatic illnesses,
I had discovered a black-and-white photo of a man's hands bloody
with nail holes. Stigmata. As the book explained, the man so identified with Christ that his hands had begun to bleed.

"What do you mean, we don't believe in Jesus?" I asked Mother.

"I guess we think he was a good person, but not God. If you want
a real explanation, you should ask your father."

As usual, Mother wasn't confident about her answers to such
philosophical speculations; nevertheless, she had glimpsed my
lonely pain, and had concocted our own reparative holiday event.
The night was clear, and the street, whose storefronts I passed every
Saturday morning on my way to my violin lesson, seemed utterly
transformed—a place of dazzling dreams. Even the corner of my
violin teacher's dreary block was festooned with jewels of light.
Cold and elated, we reached Tenth Street, the end of the four-block
business district. It was long past our bedtime, but Mother had
planned one more treat for us: in the restaurant of the Jayhawk
Hotel, we sipped cups of hot chocolate through a float of whipped
cream—our own *Schlagsahne*—as we looked out at the dark shimmering night. How perfect, how rich in wonder the world seemed
as our stomachs warmed to the hot sweet drink. If my life was finally reaching the enchantment of my mother's Berlin childhood, I
also felt like a grown-up, whiling away the late night hour.

Barbara was getting sleepy, though, and needed to be carried as
we retraced our steps to the bus. This time, we walked on the other
side of the street, which was now icy in spots from the night wind.

"Which side of the street is better, Mother?" I wanted us to compare and evaluate.

"I think the other side," she said.

I agreed: it held the two department stores, with their panoramic
windows in which the Christmas story was displayed with wooden
or clay figures and a straw manger; but on this side was an entirely
new array of radiant shop windows, and I could look across the street

to remember myself walking in the opposite direction an hour earlier. Still, I wanted to know the reason behind her preference.

"Maybe because I was feeling fresher then," Mother said wearily.

But I was high with rapture: no longer an uncertain outsider, but someone who strode along the icy pinnacle of a glistening holiday night.

CONTRARINESS MAY BE a natural part of growing up, for it is in the arguments between your thoughts and mine, what you like and I dislike, that a child senses her independence. Yet in my family, disobedience was fraught. My mother believed that, as Jewish children in a gentile land, we had to be well-behaved, showing the Christians around us that Jews were polite, modest, and well-mannered. But my father made it clear that obedience to a regime that had turned murderous was what had trapped his father and led to such massive victimization of Jews in Europe.

I must have begun early to side with my father in my contrariness, for at three years old, I had informed my parents that, "I don't have to, even if I want to." And the many times this was repeated back to me, in laughter, annoyance, and exasperation, probably increased my obstinacy. Still, I felt I was saving myself by refusing to agree or compromise. As a thick branch suddenly divides into two that each go their own way, I could feel a widening wedge between my mother and me, even when I wanted to be obedient or see things as she did. Even when I was unsure of my own view, I was moodily silent or inarticulate in my opposition to her. And then I began more and more, always with an uneasy conscience, to insist on my own darker sense of things, a vision that was increasingly influenced by my father's, although I often found cause to argue with him.

"See, Kurt says they use their scientific knowledge to grow orange trees in Israel!" Mother looked up from the pale blue aerogramme she had just received from her favorite cousin, Kurt Stern, who was building a new life as a banker in Haifa.

"In the desert?" I asked, suspicious of her feats of human progress.

"Of course! Without the Jews, it would still all be sand."

This was long before I understood the problem of lowering underground water tables, but I knew my father thought we Jews had been wrong to take Arab land. "Maybe the other people still want desert," I said grumpily.

Mother looked bewildered. "You think Arabs don't want delicious oranges?"

"People don't always like to eat new things." I was ready to list the American foods she didn't like.

"You're right," she shook her head, bewildered. Oh, what a troublesome child she with her sunny nature had somehow been saddled with raising!

One day I carried my arguments a step too far, for suddenly Mother's face was swollen with irritation. "Why do you always focus on the negative? If you want to find what's wrong with everything, you will make yourself a very unhappy young lady." Exactly how I provoked her angry warning, I can't say, though it must have been building all those times when, by pointing out a defect or a snag in her story, I seemed perversely to draw a rain cloud over her clear sky.

Was she right—about the unhappiness I could have avoided? And would I have been able to inherit her contentment and cheer, if only I had agreed to see things her way? Because neither of my parents spoke of the differences between them—indeed, Mother would have said that she always agreed with my father—I was long out of the house before I came to recognize the irreconcilable conflicts in many of their views.

If my mother ignored the darker lessons my father had drawn from the *Nazizeit*, and refused to comment directly on his rage and gloom, she used her older sister Margot as her object lesson for the wages of a critical and depressive mind. Here in the United States, Margot had reluctantly married a Sephardic Jew, a musicologist she had put off in Berlin, when she still hoped for a more romantic partner and a more comfortable life. Hermann Sawady had arrived in the United States in late 1939, and by the time I was born he was back in Germany in a U.S. uniform. With the war over, they were living near the University of Chicago, where Hermann had found a job as a music librarian.

Despite the shock treatments Margot received to combat her depression, she had periods during which she grew listless, brooding over her husband's meager income and their shabby apartment in an ugly windy city that she saw as having little to offer compared with Berlin. One cold winter, we took the train from Topeka to Chicago, and climbed the dark narrow stairs to Margot and Hermann's apartment. My aunt's unkempt hair and slack jaw made it hard to imagine her as the beautiful older sister who had been destined for a glamorous marriage in Germany.

But, unlike Margot, I didn't expect a privileged life—which was the other lesson Mother drew from her sister's illness. "If you have three pairs of shoes, what are you going to do if a war comes and you suddenly have to go without?" Whatever my desires, Mother threatened war to discipline them. Although I believed that I had my war coming, I took a victorious pleasure in imagining that, when my war occurred, my suffering would be greater than my mother's had been. (Sensing how much greater her fortitude and physical strength were than mine, I was also afraid.) Most important, if Margot hated the squalor of her American life, I was energized by roughing up smooth surfaces and exposing the dark and threatening hidden layers.

In my side yard on Lindenwood, next to Mother's vegetable garden, I began to dig to China. This dig was not a mission of international friendship, though I knew exactly how I would shake hands with the Chinese boy in his coolie hat who happened to stop to watch me emerge, head first, from the soil, in a valiant and intrepid act of rebirth. Rather, my trip through the center of the earth to its other side would expose me to the deeper inexplicable nature of all things. I would pass the roots of those wild forces that my parents and their Jewish friends had witnessed in Europe, and, though I would remain unscathed, I would emerge from my trip with this critical and esoteric knowledge. Going down through the earth also seemed the most direct route to landing as far away from Topeka as possible. In China, as I had learned, people didn't know about Jesus or celebrate Christmas. There I would choose whether or not I wanted to mention that my parents were Jews who had fled Europe.

After several days, my father came out to see the result of my digging. I lay down my shovel and sat on my mound of soil; my forehead was wet from the hot sun.

"It looks like you have a way to go before you arrive at the molten center." His lips spread into an ironic smile as he studied the hole I had dug.

"What does molten mean?"

"The center of the earth is still burning, like logs or coals that are red with heat."

If the earth got that hot, this seemed a problem: would my shovel melt? "How do you know?" I demanded.

My father said this information was available in geology books; and as usual, he offered to take me to the library. But had the geologists been down there? He shook his head no. Then I'd be the first, and I could tell them if their books were wrong. Already I was imagining my fame. My father poked at my excavation with his sandal.

"Science has ways of understanding things indirectly," he said. I didn't feel like asking how, and stood up to continue my dig as my father went indoors.

I wasn't someone for whom physical exertion comes naturally: it was more that the fantasy of deliverance had been kept alive by my shovel cutting into the soil. Still, my father's information had its power: I could feel my faith wearing away, and soon afterward I put down my shovel.

My intelligence wasn't, in fact, of that optimistic, expansive nature that wants to ferret out the truth in all things. I wasn't the kind of child whose enthusiastic curiosity about our mysterious and beautiful natural world is the sign of a biologist or a cosmic physicist in the making. The rocks I collected during our two August weeks in Colorado were arranged on top of my bookshelf, but only some had labels. It was the same with astronomy: my father had bought me a book of the constellations, but I needed him to go outside with me to look up at the stars and help me find the patterns we'd seen in the book. My own passion for knowledge and truth was inconstant. My mother was right: I was more interested in showing what was bad than what was good about the world. Good felt precarious, untrustworthy, easily false; but bad had a reassuring ring, signaling a reality that wasn't clearly talked about, and offering the possibility of a kind of relief.

THERE WAS, TO start, Mother's tale of my birth as the culmination of an exotic romance. My father never talked about that unsettled period of traveling from Vienna to London to Honolulu, and back to mainland U.S.A. in search of a place to put down new roots.

In 1939, having lived in the busy home of her Orthodox relatives for two years, Mother took a job with a Jewish self-help committee that was providing housing and care for Jewish children arriving from Austria, Germany, and Czechoslovakia on the *Kindertransport*. Thousands of children, whose parents lacked the money or visas to leave their countries, were being allowed into Britain. In unused seaside cabins outside the town of Lowestoft, on the east coast of England, my mother was placed in charge of a dozen girls. Some were Orthodox Jews. Others had grown up as Catholics, or hadn't known they were Jews until their mothers packed their rucksacks and took them to the train station, and they were panicked and revolted by their discovery. "That's why I always say you have to know that you're Jewish," my mother would pause to make clear the moral of this part of her tale.

In a nearby cabin filled with Jewish boys, the counselor was an Austrian Jew, a handsome teacher and a psychoanalyst ten years her

Irma (top row) with her boys from the Kindertransport.

senior—which was where their love story began, for Paul Bergmann (said my mother) first noticed her when the head of the Jewish self-help committee wanted to move around children and counselors, and she, Irma, argued against it. The children had already been torn from their families, and didn't know if they would ever see their parents again. One little boy, who had refused to let his blind father be dragged away alone, had even spent time in a concentration camp.

Paul and Irma began to use their breaks to take long walks along the sea. When scarlet fever broke out, the refugee children were taken in ambulances to a nearby hospital and quarantined; to prevent contamination, even their letters to their parents in Austria and Germany were burned. "How could the English be so rigid and cruel as to prevent news from reaching their parents in such terrible times!" Mother exclaimed, her eyes momentarily wet with memories of the epidemic. "But, you see, the English didn't really understand what was happening in our countries." When Paul's boys came home from the hospital, he decided that they needed a sympathetic woman to care for them, and he asked the Jewish committee to transfer Irma to his house, which was how they had become parents to a household of displaced children even before they were married.

"But weren't you scared?" I asked, sensing that mystery of adult coupling, as I snuggled deeper under the covers. For it was on those days when childhood diseases confined me to bed that she filled my empty hours with her stories.

"Yes, surely! But how else would I know if we were suited for each other?" Mother glowed with the confidence of having made exactly the right choice.

Yet the mysterious excitement of their romance also suggested paradoxes I couldn't yet articulate. The first, which I glimpsed from my father's reluctance to tell the story, was how a happy ending could be drawn from the devastation that had flung them together in a strange land. But the second was the treacherous underside of my mother's story: for at my father's beckoning, my mother had abandoned the girls under her charge, squandering the very maternal concern that had made her attractive to her lover, and that she still proudly claimed when she talked to me.

DURING OUR YEARS on Lindenwood, my father and I often walked past our first Topeka neighborhood on our way to stand at the banks of the Kansas River. As we paused in front of the white farm house where Barbara had been born when I was three, he recalled the willful child I had been so early in life. It was the kind of reminiscence I liked, for it reassured me that, as young as I was then, I already had my own story. But the little recollection also had a point.

"Why do you think you are so contrary?" my father might begin, his tone detached, curious, comforting—irresistible.

Folding my fingers inside his wonderful large warm hand, we continued on our way to the river. I probably contradicted my father less frequently than I did my mother; at least, I listened to his opinions more respectfully. My mother was pained by my contrariness, as he explained: Why did I provoke such a warm and good-hearted woman? To him, it didn't make sense.

"Do you argue with your teachers in school?"

"No, I only talk when the teacher calls on me," I said, eager for approval. I didn't tell him that sometimes I waved my hand frantically, and that I sat in front so that I would be sure to be seen, and I didn't say—it was something he knew—that I didn't have a friend.

As tears slid down my cheeks, he squeezed my hand. After a while he handed me his white handkerchief. So here was another problem—-something to work on, he suggested thoughtfully: like an out-of-balance teeter-totter that is stuck high in the air at one end and dragging on the ground at the other, perhaps I could find a way to lift one side and drop the other, to be nicer with my mother and more sociable in school.

IN 1939, MY father was in England on a transit visa while he awaited a permanent visa from a wealthy Hawaiian woman who had been psychoanalyzed in Vienna. (Hawaii was a U.S. protectorate then, not yet a state.) The visa arrived six weeks after he met my mother. To ensure that she would be able to follow him to Hawaii, he asked her to marry him before he left.

My mother remembered sending her older sister Gerda, who was living in London, the money to come to Lowestoft to meet Paul before she took such a rash step. But Gerda was in dire financial straits, and she used the money for rent or food, for which my mother never quite forgave her, and the marriage took place without the affirmation of a family member.

After weeks of travel by boat to New York, a Greyhound bus to the West Coast, and another boat to Hawaii, my father was temporarily settled in Honolulu. But for him, Hawaii was an island of lava, whose palms and hibiscus were vegetation too strange to be comforting. He cleaned toilets at the local YMCA before going off to act as a counselor in several Honolulu schools. When my mother

Paul and Irma—now Ellen—in Hawaii on Lei Day, 1940.

arrived six months later, she found the island a lush refuge and took pride in her happy genius at opening her new husband to its tropical splendor. The newlyweds lived in a shack on the beach, which my father remembered as ugly and primitive and my mother recalled as charmingly open to the balmy salt breezes.

I was conceived during a night of anguished joy, whose story I know only from my mother.

By November 1940, all seven Ascher sisters and brothers were out of Germany: Gerda was still in London, Julius in Istanbul, Manfred in Lisbon, and Gerhard had last been heard from near Valencia. (He was in prison on the Spanish/French border.) Heinz, who had found refuge in Mexico City, was working in a factory whose owner provided the necessary visas and lent the money for tickets to bring

Gertrude and Heinrich Ascher from Germany to Mexico. Leaving with their allotted ten marks apiece and a single large trunk, my grandparents traveled in a sealed train across Russia to Vladivostok, and then by boat to Japan, where they boarded a Japanese ship for Hawaii. They were to dock briefly in the Honolulu Harbor, before setting out for the Panama Canal, and from there up the eastern coast to Veracruz, where Heinz would come to meet them. But two months earlier, Japan had become an Axis power by signing the Anti-Commintern Pact with Germany and Italy. Although the

Ellen with her parents aboard ship in the Honolulu harbor.

United States was still officially neutral, it was already building its arms for war. Ignoring Hitler's campaign against the Jews, the least of which included a large "J" stamped across my grandparents' German passports, U.S. policy was to treat German Jews as Germans— and the Aschers were on a Japanese boat.

For several hours, my grandparents stood at the rail of their steamer, forbidden to disembark in Honolulu. It seemed that they would be forced to leave without embracing the daughter to whom they had said goodbye three years earlier, or meeting their new Austrian son-in-law. Finally, permission was granted for my parents to spend two hours on the boat. In a fever of excitement, my mother packed a lunch and made a lei of orchids for each parent. A black-and-white photograph shows my mother with her parents, my grandfather noticeably thinner, the leis draped over their European clothes.

At least, they were together, and mother's parents were getting to know Paul. Before the boat set sail, her father had blessed their recent marriage and welcomed his new son-in-law to the Ascher family. Mother's happiness, her frenzied relief at this brief reunion was so great that I was conceived that night as her parents' ship moved silently out of the Honolulu harbor.

"That's why I say, you were made in Hawaii," Mother liked to conclude her romantic story.

But I knew the story had another chapter. A few months later, after their boat had traveled down to the Panama Canal and up to Veracruz on the east coast of Mexico, they were met by their son, Heinz, who took them by bus to Mexico City. Having traveled more than half way around the world to find safety, my grandfather was already debilitated by displacement and loss, and he soon caught malaria and died shortly thereafter.

MY MOTHER'S RESILIENCE has become clearer to me with each passing year. While she sometimes described herself as "a Pollyanna," or admitted to seeing things through "rose-colored glasses," she must have sensed the enormous value, if not the price, of her good spirits. Though I sometimes tried to get her to see the less cheerful side of things, I could tell that, deep down where it mattered, she didn't really agree that it was better to look at the world without a rosy tint. Despite her moments of gentle self-mockery, she would soon be espousing the same positive, optimistic views with slightly altered examples, which made my guilt for the pain my criticisms caused her more complex, since like a knife carving water, the hurt seemed transient, almost without effect.

And in her way, Mother did see the cruel and the unjust. It was she, not my father, who took in the son of a neighbor when his mother was away at court each day for divorce hearings. And it was she who joined Topeka's school desegregation campaign when she understood that the children of what we then called Negroes were forced to attend separate, far shabbier public schools than the all-white school my sisters and I took for granted. (That campaign would rise to the Supreme Court, where in 1954 it would become *Brown v. Board of Education of Topeka*, the decision that ended legally segregated public education.)

Still, even her concern for others could irritate me. "Mother, they can take care of themselves," I would point out, my heart temporarily hardened. She halted, and there was a slight shake of her head, as if a fly were buzzing around her ear. But a moment later, she turned back, a smile brightening her face, "I'll just find out how they are on the telephone. You'll see, they'll be pleased!"

Did I sense that her good spirits floated on the trials of others, each one giving her a comparison by which to count herself lucky? Or did I glimpse how she rushed to repair the cracks in the world, as if with a little warmth here and some reparative glue there she could retrieve the happy security she remembered from her Berlin childhood? And did I want her to face her own petty cruelties, as much as her loss and grief? How useless and unkind a project that now seems!

FIVE MONTHS BEFORE Honolulu's Pearl Harbor was demolished by Japanese bombers, my parents took the boat from Hawaii to San Francisco, and then boarded an eastbound Greyhound to Cleveland, retracing the trip each had made separately. My father was to study at Western Reserve University for the social work degree that he hoped would enable him to practice psychoanalysis in the United States.

Yet if my parents were safely together and beginning to work towards a sensible life in the United States, a great deal was still difficult and in doubt. The disaster in Europe was widening. Gerhard was now clearly missing. (Rescued by Quakers, he was temporarily working on an apple farm in northern England, but he would soon be sent to a camp for Germans—including both Nazis and Jews—in northern Canada.) London, where Gerda had just had a son with another German Jewish refugee, was being rained upon by German bombs. And my father, who, having borrowed, saved, and finally sent tickets to get his parents out of Austria, had received news from Vienna of his father's sudden death in a *Gruppenwohnung*, or group home for Jews. Other relatives, aunts and cousins, were still in Germany and Austria, and Hitler had invaded Holland, the country to which several cousins and their families had fled.

All this must have made my birth three months later an extraordinary, if uncertain and frightening event. ("Oh no, dearie, we were so thrilled to have you!" I hear my mother's cheerful rebuttal.) The half-dozen tiny black-and-white photographs of that first year show a baby who looks worried and uncomfortable. Yet how relaxed could any baby be when asked to balance years of dislocation and the deaths of both my parents' fathers?

I was their American child, a sign of renewal in an alien land. At least they could acknowledge their successful escape and give testimony to their gratitude. I was named Carol, after Carol Ross, a minister's wife who had generously cared for them in Hawaii. If my name would give me an eerie sense of disguise as a Jew, it would also root me, as it would them, in that tropical interlude when they were no longer Europeans but had not yet been allowed on the U.S. mainland.

I was barely three when the first photos of starved concentration camp inmates appeared in the copy of *Life* magazine on our living room coffee table. Perhaps the photos made an impression; perhaps my parents kept them away from me. Yet by the time I was seven or eight, photos of emaciated human beings in striped pajamas were part of what I knew, echoing the stories I heard from refugee analysts who, having survived the camps or in hiding, had joined us in Topeka at the end of the war to begin their new lives.

One day I asked Mother how many of our relatives had died. She seemed to know the answer, but was reluctant to tell me. She shut her eyes, as if her disclosure would itself spread the crime. "Anyway, the Aschers and Oppenheimers were big families."

I never asked my father what happened to Bergmanns or Rotholtzes, his mother's family. With the exception of a beloved cousin, who had immigrated to Australia, the survival or death of his larger circle of relatives was never mentioned by either of my parents.

4

The Hare and the Tortoise

A
S THE ONLY JEWS IN OUR Kansas elementary school, Barbara and I should have felt a stronger kinship; but we rarely stood unified against the world, as some sisters did—those who dressed like twins and held hands during recess, even though they were as many years apart as we. Except for our handmade clothes, which were never quite in style, any two girls picked at random could have looked as much like sisters as we did. True, we both had brown hair and gray-green eyes, but while I had a redhead's nervousness about the sun, Barbara's thick hair, two shades darker than mine, was harmonious with her rich olive skin. I was also sure that her strong features never disappeared when she studied herself in the mirror, as mine could do, for her eyes were offset by dark lashes, and she had full cheeks and a rosebud mouth that went sulky or determined when she thought she might not get her way. Of course we played together at home; but our games were plagued by irritation, disappointment and suspicion, at least on my side. One false move, and: "Barbara's cheating!" "Mother, she won't let me . . ." If my tone was wounded virtue, Barbara's had the sly pleading of the younger sister, who had assumed all routes to victory were closed off but suddenly saw the possibility of an end run. Sometimes I thought I caught a smile she wasn't quick enough to hide.

"Having sisters helps children learn to share," Mother liked to explain to me, as if she had brought Barbara into our family a week before my third birthday to improve my moral fiber. Yet if I was easily meek with other children in the neighborhood and at school, I had a ruthless competitive streak I couldn't always rein in when it came to Barbara.

Born in August 1944, Barbara was said to give all the pleasures of a second child: she was a relaxed and contented infant—easy to care for, not as I had been. And she was growing into a happier, more resilient child than I—the kind of little girl whose warm dimpled fingers would feel reassuring in a mother's hand. Where I was shy, insecure but snappish, a perpetual alien who alternated between gloom and self-mockery at my discomfort, Barbara moved gregariously and with confidence both inside and beyond our house. While my antennae were tuned to my parents' hushed and tense conversations about what had happened to Jews in their homelands, as the second child Barbara turned her back on all this unsettling darkness. As if the rolling wheat fields that surrounded Topeka had inserted a resistant strain into her genes, she was not to be trapped by a receding tragedy she could do nothing about. Robust and stalwart, she would be our family's first real American.

THAT HOT AUGUST day when I was six, my special birthday lunch had been brought outside to a spot in our backyard by the sumac bushes. Although family vacations usually coincided with my birthday, a couple of Lindenwood children were there, and my mother's brother, Manfred, who had survived the Hitler years as a photographer in Portugal, was visiting from his new home in Detroit. Manfred had already showed me the "roving O" that enabled him to adapt wherever he might be forced to flee: in Portugal, he had become Manfredo Ascher. But if he ever had to immigrate to Ireland, his O would migrate, and presto! He would become Manfred O'Ascher, the Irishman.

With the serving platter of uneaten sandwiches still on the table, Mother had brought out my chocolate birthday cake with its six candles, when Barbara reached across her plate to stick her forefinger into the middle of my cake. That was it: one minute I was gazing expectantly at the beautifully frosted chocolate cake I had anticipated for days; the next it was destroyed! Manfred's uncanny photograph, one of the first of my family taken in color, though blanched with the years, still captures the moment. My mother's strong profile fills the foreground, her thick chestnut hair swept up with combs to keep her neck cool. Beyond her, to the right, a pudgy little girl with dark curls around her damp chipmunk face leans forward intently, having raised herself up from her chair, as she plunges her chubby finger into the dark frosting. On the far side of the table, my hair is pulled sharply back into pigtails that stick out from my pale face, and my eyes are closed with dizzying grief. Destroyed! Manfred, who could reposition us over and over, just as he did the letters of his name, to create a natural and charming family, must have rejoiced at his speed in capturing the moment.

But for me the cake was destroyed, its demise horrible! Mother reprimanded Barbara, and then quickly ran her knife over the hole in the frosting.

"See Carol, you can't even tell," she said. But I was resistant to her coercive cheerfulness.

DISCIPLINED ABOUT ADAPTING to the language of their new country, my mother and father transmitted daily facts and instructions in a grammatical but stiff English whose heavy reliance on the present tense was a direct translation from German.

"I make sauerbraten for dinner. Do you eat it with peas or spinach?"

"Spinach, please. What time do you pick me up?" This was my father, after they finally bought the dark green Pontiac Mother could use during the day if she drove him to and from Menninger.

Yet despite their determination to make English serve their utilitarian needs, the house was filled with German, as they appealed to each other, soothed or reproached my grandmother Antonie, discussed politics with my father's refugee colleagues, or gave their points extra richness and weight with a pithy adage in their mother tongue.

"*Carol, was tust du heute Nachmittag?*" What are you doing this afternoon? Someone might say, unaware that the language wasn't English.

I felt obstinate and cowardly not answering in German, but *Deutsch* sat awkwardly in my mouth, as if coated with longings and horrors that weren't mine to claim. Barbara, however, simply refused German, with its subtler gloomier passions and complexities of regret. She might head for the sink in answer to Grandmother Antonie's, "*Kind, gibst mir bitte etwas Wasser.*"

But she could also stand rooted as she demanded, "I don't know what you want. Speak English," and stared at the empty glass Grandmother held out to her.

"Barbara the barbarian!" my father called her, his r's thickened by the Austrian sounds in his speech.

Perhaps Barbara had just said no—no, she didn't want to join him on his weekly trip to the public library—and his straight dark hair had fallen momentarily over his sad, quixotic gray eyes as he shook his head. But an instant later, watching her lash on her roller skates to join the neighbor girl who was waiting on the sidewalk below, he smoothed back his hair as an amused smile lit his face at having such a robust and apparently uncomplicated stranger in our midst. Actually, he seemed pleased to loosen his reins with Barbara, to let her be a half-caste, a wild child, an American.

As for me, I could only say yes, yes: whatever he'd planned for me, I wanted to do it. I relished my time with him, and if Barbara didn't want to come, so much the better! Yet if merely standing at his side suffused me with a warmth I can still feel, being his steady ally meant stepping on a treadmill whose speed was always set just

Barbara (right) and I in 1947, wearing Mother's handmade dresses.

ahead of my pace. Did I read my schoolbook with ease? Then how about trying the Sinclair Lewis novel he had read in German in Vienna? Was I relaxing on the floor by the big radio console, listening to a sonata? Then I should listen carefully, and tell him whether it was Haydn or Schubert, and what made me think so. Absorbing my father's strict European cultural standards exposed the narrow limits of my teachers' knowledge, but it also made the children Barbara played with so freely, even becoming the leader of the pack, bland or boorish, mediocre, and frightening in their rowdy habits. At the same time, my growing sense of being different left me with an eerie inadequacy. (If my father found baseball an insipid and boring American game, it was still baseball that I had to play during recess or on weekends with the neighborhood children.) Like a captive in a fortress whose key lay hidden far across the Atlantic, I watched Barbara clatter down the front steps on her skates, for inside our family I also lived in two discordant worlds: that of a vanished

Europe I felt compelled to inherit, and the American world that Barbara's daily acts of apparently carefree independence encouraged me to adopt reluctantly for myself.

I see Barbara running across the lawns on Lindenwood, a trail of children at her heels: she is a stocky little girl with strong features whose expressions shift from bossy or raucous to pouting. Like any budding politician, she is kept busy recruiting and giving pep talks and asking for endorsements and loyalty oaths. "C'mon, let's go," she commands, and the children happily obey. Proposing an alternate critical view, which is second nature to me, irritates and confuses her: she grows silent and sullen, even tongue-tied—then runs off to her faithful troops.

"I don't know what you mean," she says, looking stubborn and opaque, after I have confided in excited tones that Mother is being friendlier to Grandma Antonie's friend, Mr. Eckstein, than she really feels.

Generally uninterested in the subterranean conflicts that absorb me, Barbara rarely joins my lonely rebellions. Even when we are under the same daily yoke, she resists my complaints that Mother has been unfair—really, to both of us! "She shouldn't make our sandwiches on pumpernickel, when everyone else at school has white bread," I might point out, unable to engage her in my logic. Nor can I draw her into resisting our father's demand that we practice our instruments for forty-five minutes every evening.

"C'mon, I'm not opening my violin case. Really! If you refuse to touch your flute . . ." I urge.

Had I lost the chance for solidarity by nastily pointing out that my violin was a harder instrument to master than her flute—reminding her that I intended to keep my edge? And did she understand that I was unlikely to give up my father for her, a mere little girl? Or was her geography simply more practical than mine, making her see quite clearly that the receding European past with its high culture and brutality, which I both resisted and clung to, would never serve her well in the immediate world she wanted to inherit?

At times Barbara did agree to my confidences and proposals. "Okay," she surprised me then, as she eagerly got up to follow me. And if the moment's high pleasure depended on its singularity, I was nevertheless in rapture, feeling that my narrow spit of territory had increased and grown more solid, for my sister was with me.

A BOOK MOTHER read to us in Topeka still sits on my shelves, its green cover long faded and cracked. Inside, impressionistic strokes in red, yellow, green, violet, and orange bring cheer to a pathetic tale about a farm donkey, mortified by his ears. Imitating the cow with whom he shares the barnyard, he sticks his ears out on the side— until one day he tears an ear on a rusty nail hanging from the barn door. Then, sure that the pig has the prettiest ears, the donkey turns his own toward the front; but they block his vision, and he rams into the ladder on which the farmer is standing to paint his house. Over and over, the donkey's abject imitation of the other farm animals ends in disaster.

I see myself sitting beside Mother's soft lap, Barbara at her other side. We are both quiet and attentive, for we love these half-hours when Mother puts aside her chores to read us a story, and we have learned from our father that books are windows onto mystery and wisdom. Whether Barbara finds a lesson in the donkey's trials, I can only surmise. Perhaps she identifies instead with the other farm animals, each happy to demonstrate that his ears hang the right way. For she understood early what it would take me decades to glimpse: that one can turn whoever one is—introspective or athletic, Christian or Jew—to advantage.

As for me, though I listen raptly to all the masochistic turns in the donkey's abject imitation, I grow impatient as we reach the final pages where a little sparrow, perched on a nearby fence, offers his kindly advice. "Donkey, donkey, silly donkey. You aren't a dog. You aren't a lamb. You aren't a pig. You are a donkey. Keep your ears up as donkeys do."

Do I believe in such simple self-acceptance—of myself as a Jew with European parents, or simply as a little girl who is both eager to understand everything and would like to hide from sorrow and complication? No. Never.

MY FATHER'S COLLEAGUES at the Menninger Sanitarium could have offered strong enough examples of secular Jews thriving on their idiosyncrasies. Yet something had gone wrong: though being surrounded by outlandishness in both analysts and patients seemed to give a push to Barbara's brazen self-possession, in me it encouraged conformity, timidity, and politeness—broken by moments of unmoored rebellion and humiliating rage.

The sanitarium sat on former farmland by the cemetery, at the edge of town. On the east side of Sixth Street, a large farmhouse and several other structures housed the very ill patients. On the west side, a new one-story pinkish building contained the dark hushed offices where both residential and out-patients had their treatment hours. After we bought the Pontiac, Barbara and I often rode out with Mother to pick up our father in the evening. Sitting in the car, we would watch a male patient walking slowly across the wide lawn, his hands clasped behind his back as he muttered to himself, or a gaudily dressed woman with an attendant, whose hand resting lightly on her elbow suggested the potential for erratic behavior, even escape. Sometimes Mother let us leave the car to go into the treatment center. Then, if the receptionist said, "Dr. Bergmann is free now," I would take Barbara's hand and race down the long dusky hall in a cold terror at the wretchedness behind every closed door.

"You're hurting me," she inevitably complained. "Why are you going so fast?"

Several days a week, my father also treated patients at the Southard School, a home for delinquents, and at the state hospital, both located on Sixth Street, between our house and Menninger. While the Southard School looked like an ordinary large white farmhouse, the state hospital buildings were behind a stone wall, invisible from the street, and the Gothic construction had heavily barred windows and screened-in porches through which shadowy figures cried out in spurts of desperation and unearthly rage.

As a doctor at the state hospital, my father was entitled to a small kitchen garden at the edge of the hospital grounds, on unused land by the Kansas River. On warm summer evenings, I would be tying up the tomatoes, my parents crouched at other vegetables a few rows away. Once, a patient in baggy hospital pajamas, as emaciated as a concentration camp victim, stood watching me with hollow eyes.

"Hello," I forced myself to whisper, dry-mouthed with fear.

But Barbara had what Mother called "a natural friendliness." Like Mother, she saw herself as enhancing her good fortune by helping others. Snapping off a tomato or pulling a carrot from the dirt, she offered her vegetable to the patient. "Here, do you want something really fresh?"

If my father's profession allowed me to glimpse the extremity of private suffering, he was also suggesting that the finest thread separated me from both children and adults whose minds had snapped and who had been put away. Like them, I had an unconscious, which could suddenly shoot forth weird thoughts or embarrassing acts, or even make me forget things I ought to have known. Through both his calm mesmerizing descriptions of the anger or guilt burdening a patient he was treating, and his analysis of how I was being "defensive" or "acting out," my father gave me my first understanding of human psychology.

But unlike the miner who brings gold and diamonds to the earth's surface, my father's careful prying exposed immaturity, ugly emotions, and raw nerves. Even the innocent "A" I earned in school by being careful with my penmanship, obeying my teacher's instructions, and remembering what she had taught, could become a

source of shame, suggesting that I was too controlled, even obsessive. I must have been ten or eleven when I showed him a social
studies paper, hoping for his affirmation. But, shaking his head with
concern, my father said, "Sadly, your intellectual success has come
at the expense of your social development." So this too was something I had to recognize in myself, and wonder how to change.

It was likely my father who would later remark that, although
Barbara's grades weren't as good as mine, she was a better person:
warmer, more generous and forgiving. Or was this just one of the
conclusions I had drawn, like finding medical bills and understanding that there has been some quiet tragedy?

BARBARA AND I had the long blue room at the head of the stairs, its
windows opening toward both the side yard and the street—though
I was never an easy roommate, and we were ill suited to sharing
space. Tidiness may have been my route to control, but I liked to display my rock collection on the smooth top shelf of our bookcase,
and to arrange the tiny furniture in the wooden dollhouse Mother
had built for us. But Barbara was like the tornado on the horizon of
a wheat field I had seen from our car window. I would come upstairs
to my room—our room—perhaps to make my doll a new outfit
with some scraps of material from Mother's sewing drawer. What
faced me would be a tumult of Barbara's belongings.

"Barbara!" I screamed.

Each time, Mother firmly marked off our separate sides of the
room: there was a rug, then a chair, and finally a bookcase to make
the edge clear: Barbara and her possessions were to stick to her side.
But I should have remembered that a tornado respects no human
boundaries. Sometimes when I stamped and raved, Barbara looked
up with sorrowful eyes. "I didn't mean to," she said, belatedly using
my language of intention and responsibility.

Who can say what differences, great or small, might have
emerged between us under other circumstances; for neither his-

tory, nor temperament, nor birth order can ever be replayed. Moreover, both our parents were as active in delineating our contrasts as they were in stimulating the suspicion and rivalry that seemed to grow between us each year. It was as though, despite their temperamental differences—my mother's sturdy optimism faithfully blooming with each of my father's dark moods—they had agreed to hedge their bets by investing in two divergently trained horses. Or perhaps their unstated agreement was that they each would train one of us. But the race horse analogy is mine. Mother's similes were different:

"Carol is like an old watch, elegant, but always breaking down," I overheard her say one morning to another refugee. "But Barbara is a Timex. No fuss, reliable."

What! Barbara more reliable than I? Though ear infections and stomachaches often kept me home from school, how could Mother ignore that it was I who day after day put the games away in their correct boxes and the doll clothes back inside the little trunk? I, who over and over accepted the older sister's obligations of cooperation and restraint?

On our neighbor's carved wooden weathervane there was a couple, Sunny and Stormy, who came out, one or the other, depending on the weather. As with Sunny and Stormy, Barbara and I seemed linked by opposing climates. Yet it is false to say that I was always the uncomfortable introvert and she the easy sociable one. For at five or six she began to bite her nails, tearing them with her teeth each time she paused in flight, so that the tips of her fingers were fleshy and pink like gums without teeth.

"Ach, Barbara!" Mother cried. She couldn't understand why such a happy popular child, a child who gave the world such pleasure, should be so savage with herself.

MIRIAM WAS BORN in 1949, when Barbara was five and I was eight. Mother was still large with her pregnancy when Grandmother

Antonie moved into a boarding house a few blocks beyond our elementary school.

"Don't you want to keep sharing with me?" Barbara's gray-green eyes were moist at the prospect of my cool departure to the pink papered room. Though she had never wanted her own room, I don't think she realized that she was to share the blue room with the new baby.

Barbara took to spending more time outside the house, becoming a neighborhood vagabond. But having a new baby made it easier for me to stay inside and read undisturbed. Though there was an eerie anxiety about the baby not being healthy, I closed the door of the pink room whose strewn books, games, and clothes seemed cozy now that they were only mine, and lying on my bed, drank in the library books that I had chosen with my father, or the paperbacks I had ordered through the monthly book club at school: *Treasure Island, Robinson Crusoe, Kon-Tiki, The Conquest of Mount Everest*—tales about lonely explorers, or ordinary people stranded in dire circumstances, were those I loved best. They raised the questions that haunted me: under what terrible circumstances did people exchange politeness for cruelty? What happenstance or personal flaw made someone either perish or survive?

I was thirteen when *The Diary of Anne Frank* appeared in English, and all my inchoate questions about how one could be tested by the extremities of nature shifted to the cruel catastrophes people intentionally wreaked on each other. The narrative of Anne's confined and entrapped life—and terrible death—might have been mine, had my parents fled to Holland rather than England, and it gave me details with which to inflame the morbid isolation in which I was entangled. Like Anne, I confided in a father I adored and felt estranged from and misunderstood by my Mother. I too might have gone into hiding, as I knew Mother's cousins had done, unable to stretch their legs for months on end, until that moment when men in high leather boots suddenly stood over them, and even their cramped hideout became a remembered luxury. How I lay on my bed then, in a swoon of endangered solitude, communing with this fragile saucy girl whose hair was parted on the side like mine, and who had died in a concentration camp when she was my age.

A NOTE FROM my fifth-grade teacher, informing my parents that I had no friends at school, sent me belatedly scurrying down Barbara's path of sociability.

"I think you should see a therapist," my father pronounced from his living room armchair, the shameful letter still folded in his hand.

"Why?" My cheeks were burning.

"It would help you with your inhibitions."

"What do you mean?"

"I think you have too much aggression, which makes you timid . . ." he started a complicated analysis I didn't want to hear.

"Act like a father, not a psychoanalyst!" I shouted.

He blanched, and nodded sadly. "I guess I don't know how to be other than myself."

For a moment, I had no answer; then I cried out, "So why do you want *me* to change?"

Though I had succeeded in stunning my father, I felt perilously close to the inmates at Southard School and the state hospital whose forced confinement had seemed a warning about the danger of being different. Yet I had only been too quiet, too much by myself. I could barely look at my teacher, who had betrayed me with her note.

A friend!

How my inner eye roamed the other fifth graders, unable to imagine turning any of them into a friend. A friend! If I ever had a natural outgoing instinct, my attitude toward my schoolmates was now colored by fear, distaste, revulsion, as well as the certainty that the world was dangerous and that I had to disguise my natural tendencies to withdraw.

I had relied on my father too long, but he was an untrustworthy ally; the time for confiding in him was over. As for my mother, what was I to do when she knocked on my bedroom door, asking with her awful cheer if it wouldn't be nice to put down my book and call a friend? In the meantime, Barbara, by excelling so effortlessly where I had failed, had become the victor, the leader, the older one. How could I share my defeat with her? I would still live at home, but I would trust no one. I would watch the popular girls; like Barbara, I would become an American.

IT IS AFTER dinner, and Mother and Barbara are in the kitchen. As I go in and out, bringing in plates and returning food, I see them picking at the remains of a dish that Mother had announced was meant for two meals. I too could eat more, but our house is filled with so much fear and confusion about food that it is difficult to know how to eat. On the one side, Mother worries that, if we eat too well, we will be unprepared to survive when a war comes. On the other, she has noticed that American women are much slimmer than she, and she has decided that both she and Barbara should lose weight. Books and pamphlets on diets and health sit on the kitchen work area, and a calorie list is taped to the refrigerator door.

"Peas are fattening," Mother says sadly, examining her calorie guide.

She drops a tiny white saccharin tablet into her coffee. But sometimes she bakes *Butterkuchen* or *Pflaumenkuchen,* and the house fills with the warm smells of Europe and for a few hours there is no mention of diets.

TEN YEARS LATER, I was in college at Vassar, which I knew was a very good college. Although it had a quota for Jewish admissions in those years, I had been accepted, and I was getting good grades. Yet, because my adored father had both ridiculed the inadequacies of the American university and warned me that I would be among students much brighter than I, I could not use my accumulating evidence to reshape either my estimate of the education

I was receiving or of my capacity. Where I *was* becoming confident was in my ability to watch others and imitate, step by excruciating step, the rigors of American teenage popularity, for I had done just that throughout high school, even acquiring a boyfriend by graduation day.

Yet living away from home for the first time, I was letting go of the awful vigilance that had brought me to an acceptable level of sociability, and was falling back into a more isolated and scholarly self, even an ascetic self. I studied from early morning until the library closed at night. Creating my own private war, I ate little, and my hipbones poked sharply through my increasingly baggy clothes. Sensing that I was in psychological trouble, and safely away from my father, I cycled once a week to a therapist outside the college, where I spent fifty minutes sobbing with inarticulate grief.

How could I, who had never suffered from a war, complain about the vise of my refugee parents' contradictory demands and petty hurts?

Each time I came home on holiday visits, I found Barbara at a new height of popularity: she was junior varsity cheerleader, president of her senior class, voted most popular and most likely to succeed. Hearing the phone ring, Mother or Father called out with delight, "It's for Barbara!" When Barbara was at home with her friends, the sounds of laughter filled the rooms, though more often she was rushing off to a car horn on the street. But on vacation nights, when we slept in the same room again, I watched her chew her nails and heard her cry inconsolably.

One day, as she was copying a book report on *The Diary of Anne Frank*, I realized that she had been turning in the same slightly revised report for several years.

"Barbara, that's cheating!"

"My teacher will never know," she glanced up, tearing at a nail.

Perhaps *her* Anne was the perky younger sister, the prankster, who before going into hiding had always been in the midst of a gang of friends. And there were probably other reasons why tears suddenly filled her eyes as she flopped back on her bed. But I couldn't help wondering if somewhere far beneath her adolescent successes Barbara was also pulled by our family's tangled demands and complicated history.

5

My Father's Violin

WITHIN A SINGLE CONVERSATION, my father could be whimsical, caustic, tender, pedantic, and charming. "A true Viennese," as my mother liked to say, her voice trembling with awe—and sometimes an undercurrent of disdain. His lips widened in the slightest grin as he repeated a joke he had heard from a patient, made a pun, or emphasized his point with a German maxim and a thump on the arm of the chair where he was sitting.

Yet when I think of my father, I hear his voice, fury rising, as he calls across the room in response to a false note I have just played on my violin. I am eight, nine, ten years old, and have been dragging my violin downtown on the bus each Saturday morning since I was six. On a side street off Kansas Avenue, I climb a dark stairwell to a dusty studio on the second floor, where a fat dreary woman with hair like straw and stubby fingers whose nails are cut to the quick, as mine should be to move soundlessly from note to note, gives me a half-hour lesson. "In Topeka," as my father assures me, giving a whack to the arm of his chair, "when it comes to music teachers, there is only one choice." In any case, it is the intimacy between my father and me, both brutal and sweet, that fuels my erratic progress on the violin.

Most evenings, my father would be reading by lamplight at the far end of the living room while I played my violin. (If I'd been asked why I didn't avoid his rage by practicing before he came home, I would have shrugged uncomfortably while I dredged up my excuses. After school, I needed to read my library book, or to spend time outside with the other children on the street, like a normal American girl, as I had been told to do. But the truth was that I felt lonely, desolate, practicing by myself; I wanted him to hear me, his suspicious attention tracing every note I played.) When my finger landed too low on the string, or I rushed the tempo, or even let my violin droop on my tired shoulder, his leonine disgust closed the distance between us. "My God, don't you know where that note is?" A terrible loathing could issue from my father's voice. How could I, his eldest daughter, from whom he had the right to expect minimal succor, instead rub salt in his wounds? These moments were electric for me. All his bitterness and frustration, his loneliness and estrangement, were channeled into a concentrated stream as he called out, "Pitch!" or "Tempo, please. You're speeding up again!" If I couldn't be the wellspring of his happiness, I could momentarily be the source of all his disappointments, leeching his pain of emigration and exile by absorbing his terrifying sound.

Perhaps I use those harsh moments when my breath stopped in terror at having made a musical mistake to screen myself against the rush of giddy warmth that came as my father put down his book to join me at the piano. Then, as he accompanied me, I smelled the oil he used to smooth back his long dark hair, European-style. Each of us would be following his own score, but the music we made was a union of our two instruments, our four hands. Sometimes, too, after I had practiced the required forty-five minutes, and put down my violin, he would ask me to join him in the Hugo Wolf or Schubert lieder we both loved. *"Wer nie sein Brot mit tränen ass..."* (He who has never eaten his bread with tears), I would sing in my clear untrained voice, watching his square neat hands with the tiny black hairs as they moved over the keyboard. My heart swelled then, from being with my father, from the beautiful melody, and from the German, which, despite Hitler, conveyed the sounds of love.

The piano stood in the space between the glass front door and the stairway banister where my father hung those few drawings of mine or Barbara's that he judged as meriting display. I remember two large, carefully worked pictures, my first attempts at perspective, that he agreed to exhibit: a baseball stadium filled with tiny people cheering the players on the diamond, and a city corner with narrowing streets disappearing into the distance while skyscrapers lifted high into the sky. Since I had seen neither a baseball stadium nor a large city, both must have been inspired by newspaper photographs. (Later he would point out that my success with perspective, for which I relied heavily on a ruler, was a sign of repression, which would ultimately hamper my creativity.) My mother would be in the kitchen, a dusky opening beyond the stairs. Yes, the pleasure was there, for me as well as my father, in our duet. Even in the promising warm smells of cooked vegetables and meat coming from the kitchen.

But the pleasure too soon evolved into a heightened pressure to perform—and a dread of failure. Only in rare moments are we equals playing together; most of the time, I am submerging my will to his, breathless to be the musician he needs me to be. Moreover, at any instant, my violin can disobey my command or my voice can mispronounce the German, which my father, leaning into the music, will grouchily correct, his disappointment and wrath, his quick disgust with life, so near.

Besides, soon my mother will lay her hand cautiously on my father's shoulder as she reminds him once again that dinner is ready. For she came out just before we started the last piece, but my father asked for five more minutes. This time she will rebuke us that the food is getting cold.

Sometimes as we came to the end of a violin sonata in which I had done well, perhaps played quite accurately, even riding that splendid narrow channel of feeling, my mind suddenly threatened to collapse as I rushed to complete the piece, or, holding panic at bay, keeping the tempo, with the very last note came catastrophe, as my bow careened across the bridge scratchily, carelessly.

"*Ach!*" my father would exclaim, enraged, heartbroken, slamming his fists into the piano keys.

As IF MY father has come to stand behind my shoulder, I am suddenly concerned not to inflate the skill or gift I had as a child. For decades, I was besieged by anxiety at the thought of anything positive about myself. Not only was it impossible to be too modest, but the standards by which I was measured became clear only when I failed to meet them. Of course I could play the Haydn, with its simple, repeating melodies. But the Bartok or the Prokofiev—how miserable they sounded! I could hear it myself. As for the golden stars my violin teacher pasted in my music books as the culmination of my Saturday morning lessons, they only gave proof of the low level of expectations all around me. My father would have said, "Compliments are cheap," meaning that those who offered compliments were cheapened by the act, perhaps because they gave away their squalid desire to win favors by their flattery. As for my father, disappointed idealist that he was, having once imagined contributing to a world where all men (though perhaps not all women) were justly honored, compliments must have been too expensive to give.

One day at my desk on the second floor of Potwin Elementary School, I made the following calculation: if I was the smartest student in my class, which seemed probable (only Kathy, whose mother taught fifth grade, and who could imitate exactly the sloped lines of the script in our Pitman penmanship books, sometimes got better marks), and all classes in Topeka were like this class, and all cities were like Topeka, then I might just be the smartest girl in America. With a few pitiless words, my father would have promptly cut down such arrogant hypothesizing. Beyond the fact that Americans would never match the Europeans he had known, he would have made clear that the fantasy itself showed the meagerness of my understanding.

Knowing the futility of asking for praise, Barbara and I invented a little game. Our ballet teacher (the wife of a young training analyst at Menninger, who had come from New York) sometimes gave us hand-me-down dresses we thought particularly glamorous. We would stand in front of our father, wearing a dress that sat off the shoulder or whose full skirt flowed from a wide belt, demanding merely that he tell us what was new. "Is it your socks?" he glanced up, letting his book close temporarily on the emery board he used to mark his place.

Disgusted, I sucked my teeth and shook my head.

"Maybe you did something with your hair," he turned to Barbara. His eyes, which were so astute when instructing us in the richness of a painting or the meaning of a poem, had become as dull as if covered with cataracts.

I imagine there was uncertainty, even fear, in my father's harshness and his inability to praise—though all of this is surmise. He had grown up an only child of parents whose technical education and work ethic had enabled them to make a success of first a shop and later a factory, despite difficult economic times. He criticized his mother for working alongside his father, rather than staying at home to care for him. Perhaps he somehow believed that, had he been more charming or gifted, she would have found it worthwhile to be a full-time mother. Supported by psychoanalytic theory, and with little resistance from my mother, he made sure that she was a housewife who filled her days with cleaning, cooking, and sewing, and was there when we returned from school.

Certainly my father was as harsh with himself as he was with us. Over and over, he turned his searing critical intelligence on his own work, repudiating previous commitments and accomplishments wholesale. A book wasn't worth bothering to write, unless its contribution stood alongside those of the great nineteenth century theory-builders: Darwin, Freud, and Marx. Yet Marx himself had been mistaken in his outline of a just society, as the slave labor camps in the Soviet Union made clear, while Freud's great theories of the

mind were merely helping middle-class neurotics, who had money
and leisure to engage in endless introspection. Psychoanalysis,
client-centered psychotherapy, Gestalt therapy, drug therapy, even
behaviorism—my father investigated them all with initial hope and
enthusiasm, practiced each diligently but with waning conviction,
until he eventually discarded it as not good enough.

As for his own professional articles, once the dishes were cleared
from the dining room table, he labored over them for months, clar-
ifying and revising his thoughts, asking me with each new draft to
check his English for an awkwardness he might have missed, and
with all that sometimes, nevertheless, returning the piece to the oblivion of his worn cardboard file deep in his closet. "The trees they destroy for the junk they write!" my father said glumly, talking not only
of the common paperbacks in the bookshops, but of the psychoanalytic articles his less fastidious colleagues allowed into print.

THOUGH THE LITTLE table next to my father's living room chair
overflowed with the novels, essay collections and scientific studies he
was reading, his attitude toward books was that of a refugee. True, he
had carried his leather-bound German volumes through each stage
of his flight, but he was not interested, as most book lovers are, in
shelves that documented the history of his intellectual passions or
changing curiosities. "It's senseless," he would shrug. "You only have
to get rid of them when you move." What he had were library cards,
and librarians who went out of their way to track down the esoteric
books he asked for with Austrian courtesy and charm.

Which is why I still recall that warm evening at the auction house
when I was ten. My father, who liked to take after-dinner walks with
Barbara and me, often turned in that direction. We would slip onto
the benches in the outdoor back area, where the stocky auctioneer
sang out, "Who'll give me five dollars, five, five? Let's hear five. Now
who'll give me six, six? I see six." On this night a twenty-four volume
set of Balzac's novels bound in navy cloth came before the auction-

eer, who shook his head at them incredulously. But he was a sport, a man not easily undone by challenges. So, while he worked his way toward pronouncing B-A-L-Z-A-C, he reminded his audience how nice a set of blue books could look in an empty bookcase—some of them had probably paid a lot for the *Encyclopedia Britannica* for just that reason. He also flipped through one of the volumes and tried to read aloud a few lines, but the prose didn't reassure him that it would prompt an eager bid. Still, he made a little joke about entertainment on those long cold nights (this was before most people had a TV). Then he began, "Who'll give me twenty-five dollars? Now ladies and gentlemen, that's just a little over a dollar a piece." There were no takers, and the numbers started to come down. "Who'll give me twenty, twenty? Do I hear eighteen? Who'll give me fifteen, fifteen? Do I hear fifteen? Now how about ten?" I turned to my father, whose face was set in amusement, but something in his eyes appeared stricken.

"Poor Balzac," he said, as the auctioneer searched the crowd for someone who would part with five dollars.

Perhaps my father wasn't fast enough, for the auctioneer was crying, "Now, who'll give me two-fifty?" My father had barely raised his hand when the auctioneer pounced, "Sold!"

"Ten cents apiece," my father said, getting to his feet, "I should have paid more."

In the back room of the auction house, my father put down two bills and change, and the next evening we retraced our steps with our red wagon to pick up the complete set of Balzac. Though Barbara and I were jubilant, my father seemed subdued: books, as much as children, he seemed to say, implied a moral commitment. Once you had them, you didn't give them away simply because they were inconvenient. When we moved to Seattle a couple of years later, and to Bethesda, Maryland, three years after that, he packed the Balzac along with his Austrian leather-bound volumes. Loyal to his legacy, I kept the set of Balzac long after he died.

———————

THINKING ABOUT MY father as I write, brings back the old violin ache in my left shoulder, and once again I feel deprived, despairing, filled with a sullen hatred for him. Am I simply, like the negative of a long lost photo, repeating his lack of forgiveness toward his mother? And can I attribute to his legacy my recurring bouts of self-laceration and depression? The tendency to feel that, despite so many signs to the contrary, my mistakes are what count, and whoever I am is inadequate or wrong. That I easily imagine others evaluating me on the bases of my most obvious (or most hidden) weaknesses, that I have and deserve nothing of value, that I have no room to maneuver and nothing to negotiate, that whatever space I take in the world is too much, that not until I am a dot in the universe as small as a meaningless speck from my pen will I be irreproachable.

Like my father, my critical eye also lands too easily on whatever is ugly, damaged, false, stupid, deformed, filthy, or ill; and, like him, I too often revert to irritation, hopelessness, disgust.

Often when I was careening with some thrilling discovery that promised to lift me out of an obscure hurt or misery, my father would look up suspiciously from his book, his eyes barely grazing the rim of his glasses.

"I might trust what you're saying, if you could express yourself in a calm voice."

Perhaps I had wanted permission to skip practicing for one day. "Just one, Daddy! You said yourself that people often get better after a rest." Or I was desperate for some new pretty piece of clothing, like patent leather party shoes that my mother saw no use for. Sure that these shoes were the solution to being "like everyone else" and feeling comfortable with the other girls in school, I was campaigning for a bigger allowance so that I could buy them myself.

"You promised me an increase this year!"

"From my calculations, the year still has almost eleven more months."

"But everybody is going to wear patent leathers to the Valentine's Day party."

"Everybody?" He shook his head at my imprecise language.

I'm sure he would have explained that he was trying to teach me measure, perhaps even to help still the turmoil raging deep in me; but the effect was to reduce me, mortify me, send me into a tailspin of impotence and shame.

"You get excited about things *you* want," I said, stomping my feet.

"I'm talking about a desperation in your voice. It belies your certainty that patent leather shoes will solve your unhappiness," my father replied curtly.

"Everything I do is wrong!" I shouted in despair.

"Ah, but try to be a little less subjective," he would say. "You don't consider whether a sentence is true or false, but only whether it hurts you."

Although I had never been in psychoanalysis, I surmised that my father's well-aimed arrows, which also carried my first inkling of sexual degradation, were the method by which he leeched sickness from his patients, that to enter psychoanalysis was to agree to a process of shameful yet also exciting self-exposure, like suddenly looking down at myself in school to discover that I'd left home without my blouse or underpants (both recurring dreams). Sometimes, like a caged animal, I shouted back at him, "I don't want to hear your insights about me!" Then my father looked at me with a helpless grief, his gray eyes sagging behind his glasses.

"We're too much alike," he once told me sadly, when I was a teenager and we were on one of the long haunting walks we had begun to take together. I had thought that my personality was being carved, whittled down, and engraved in order to suit his desires, yet now it seemed that whoever I was becoming had been shaped out of his own confused discontent.

MY FIRST PSYCHIATRIST was an elderly refugee with thinning hair whose dusky office was on Central Park West. The year was 1965, but his sense of my natural destiny might have been Freud's: he listened for a session or two before promising to cure me of my need to pin down my thoughts with words on a page. Although I was sane enough to flee his treatment, I had long believed that all my desires stemmed from unknown destructive, perverse, and embarrassingly erotic impulses—impulses that in a better self would be erased. As a child, I had been afraid of letting on that I had the sniffles. It was unbearable to hear my mother recall, as she tucked me in, the galoshes I'd stubbornly refused to wear, against her better advice. Harder still to listen while my father, sitting down at the foot of my bed, analyzed my fear of the school picnic, or later, with Barbara our family's spectacular social success, speculated that envy of her must be making me ill. I was "hypochondriacal," he would say, diagnosing my condition, which meant that my earaches, sore throats, and upset stomachs, as well as the trouble I had falling asleep, were caused by those conflicts he had recognized but I persisted in hiding from myself by turning them into physical ailments. In short, the petty illnesses I attracted like a magnet draws hairpins were somehow false, inauthentic, and cowardly.

In the evenings when I was eleven or twelve my father began a course of treatment to decrease the tension he discerned inside me. On Grandmother Antonie's deeply colored Caucasian carpet, which had hosted my father, tears glazing his face, as he paced back and forth to a sonata by Brahms or Dvorak or a lieder cycle by Mahler, he arranged my limbs out from my body as I lay on my back. Pulling up a chair, he sat above me as he asked me to join him in hypnotizing myself. "My right arm feels heavy." I was to repeat this silently over and over, after him. "My right arm feels heavy." The point was to get my limbs, one by one, to move off beyond my control, into relaxation. "My right leg feels heavy. My right leg feels heavy." Despite my wariness, I tried to let the slack come, as my soul beneath my thin clothes lay exposed to his abstracted gaze.

THERE IS A photo of me, an eight-year-old mother in my Brownie uniform, helping Miriam take her first steps. Though I had sewn what I hoped were stylish clothes for my doll, I had never cuddled a

Miriam and I

doll or created the cozy imaginary families by which little girls are said to practice for future motherhood. My father's ever-changing points of attack made it clear that I wouldn't be a natural mother, like my own mother, or even like Barbara. (Barbara fondled an array of stuffed animals until their fur fell out from her sweaty devotion.) Besides, something was apparently wrong with Miriam. Though she was an astonishingly beautiful child with large blue eyes and curly flax-colored hair, my father had been disappointed and worried by his first glance at her through the hospital glass. Unlike the other infants in the nursery behind the window, he said, she lay motionless in her crib. She was also an unresponsive baby, in his view. He and Mother waited impatiently for her to crawl and walk and, at last, begin to speak. Even I could see that something wasn't quite right: she would come out of her eerie stillness to scream with convulsive panic if Mother tried to leave her. Sometimes when Mother had to go out, Barbara and I stood by helplessly, unable to stop Miriam's screeching, until we became exasperated, and began to hate our little sister—-when other schoolchildren were so proud of the babies in their houses—-and felt trapped by a bewildering shame.

By the time Miriam entered public school in Seattle, everything made her cringe in fear: a little traffic, other children, even meal time. What if the milk were sour? What if she swallowed a bone in the fish? For a year, my father drove her to a child psychiatrist, where she sat mutely, refusing to touch any of the toys that were supposed to help her talk her way through her difficulties. Finally the weekly torture of hope raised and dashed was stopped. Miriam also refused our father's world of art and music, often forcing

Miriam, age ten

Mother to stay home with her, rather than join the rest of us in a trip
to a museum or concert. When she was eight or nine, she developed
a facial tic—half sneer, half irritation, that momentarily snapped
shut one eye—which our father began to treat with the behavior
management techniques that then interested him. Although he had
worked his hypnotism on me on the living room rug, he took
Miriam downstairs to the office where he saw patients. I felt vaguely
critical of him for trying to treat Miriam, and I was uneasy whenever they were downstairs in the soundproofed room—especially
since I was fairly certain that he didn't really like her.

I have been able over the years to write fondly and with humor
about our émigré family by pretending that Miriam was never born.
But I have no winsome or witty way to describe the anxious pall her
presence cast over the family, making all of us seem unbalanced,
desperate, sadistic, corrupt. Sometimes it seemed that, with this last
child, the first to be given a Jewish name, we had been flung back-
wards in history, and that we ourselves had become Nazis in our in-
tolerant hate.

THE RAGE AND grief at Miriam's disabilities, which we each generally kept to ourselves, was only part of the dissolution and dislocation my family experienced after we left Topeka's close refugee
community. In Kansas, I had sensed an obscure threat of violence
from my mother's tense hand clasp whenever we stood on the curb
watching a patriotic parade; had sensed a more inward violence behind the bars of the state hospital where my father went to treat his
patients. But in Seattle, where we arrived in late August of 1953, the
borders of civility had become shifting, unreliable, often invisible.
Although my parents had now been in the United States a dozen
years, once again we were like refugees, alone and without the
proper knowledge. Why, for example, did we not understand until
too late that the lovely house on which my parents put a bid, hoping
to own a home whose large windows gave onto the Pacific Ocean,

was in a "restricted community"? Why did my parents not investigate other options when it turned out that along the street where we did buy a house students my age attended a vocational high school? Did my father assume that typing and auto mechanics were the best that American high schools óffered? Or was sending me to a vocational high school a sign of his radical egalitarianism, and his identification with the working class? Perhaps he simply decided that it didn't really matter what kind of schooling a daughter received. I'm not sure he paid more than brief attention when several years later, after learning the requirements for entering college from a rather uninterested counselor, I rushed to make up courses in algebra, geometry, and French during condensed summer sessions.

My father had taken a job in an experimental sanitarium on the outskirts of Seattle, which, anticipating R.D. Laing and other hopeful theorists of mental illness during the 1960s, attempted to cure people by allowing them to "go through" their craziness. Sanitarium patients, young and old, roamed the grounds freely, socializing with the staff, encouraged to express their upset and anger—including at my father, who twice came home with a broken nose. One rainy Sunday, a young man who had been invited to our house to share a home-cooked noon meal, hoisted himself onto our roof, where he spent the long afternoon hours, pacing and threatening to end his life, while Barbara, Miriam, and I watched in fear from the neighbor's home.

Adding to our sense of a civility careening dangerously out of control, my father, who was in communication with Timothy Leary, was experimenting with LSD. He said he hoped to find a cure for schizophrenia, which had not succumbed to other methods. Sometimes on the weekend, having taken one of the little white pills he stored in our refrigerator, he locked himself in his bedroom; then we women of the house tried to create activities to take our mind off him while we waited for late evening when he finally emerged and, sitting unsteadily at the kitchen table over a cup of tea, told us how hills had turned into breasts during his dip into mental illness.

EVEN THE MUSICAL connection my father and I had shared grew rancorous, bitter, and untenable in Seattle. Although my yellow-haired violin teacher was soon replaced by a steely angular woman who came to the house, the cross-country move had temporarily left us without a piano. Finding my pitch with a tuning fork, I set my music stand in the meaningless unmoored space of the living room and dragged alone through the forty-five minutes. Nor was there any gratification for me in my father's corrections from "the peanut gallery," as I now called his blue chair by the window. And if he wasn't at home, I was testy and quarrelsome when he asked me later how long I had practiced. Some weeks I took grim pleasure in hearing my teacher say I had progressed, when I knew that I had barely lifted the violin from its case.

Though I had dreaded the move to Seattle, I quickly saw the advantage of being in a new school where no one knew anything about me. Assuming a fresh start in my struggle for adolescent popularity, I decided that an important requirement was to know the words to the top hits—as the others on the school bus did. But my father considered rock 'n roll, which was just emerging, banal and tasteless music, and he didn't want it played on his radio. Since I had become adept at saving my allowance for American things my parents saw no need for, I must have understood that I could buy my own radio. But I seemed intent on leaving my father's radio on the rock 'n roll station, which meant proving the aesthetic value of the music. I remember my slippery victory when my father reluctantly agreed that one song, "Earth Angel", had artistic merit. I would sit with my ear to the soft-playing console to avoid my mother's complaint about the "trashy sounds," growing increasingly tense as the deejay moved up the top forty chart, because I wanted "Earth Angel" to remain high enough on the charts to be played only after he came home and could listen. But, even with this one song, his patience was short-lived, and I could never interest him in "The Great Pretender," or "In the Still of the Night."

All of this only made standing in the living room with my violin under my chin an excruciating reminder of what an outsider, a misfit, I still was—someone whom my peers in the vocational high school had every right to view as a nerd or a creep. No wonder I was tongue-tied, unable to start a conversation, when a classmate smiled at me from the next locker, where she was getting out her books! And it was worse still, when a boy seemed to slow down to walk to the next class with me! If only I played a wind instrument—this became my new campaign. I managed to convince my father to buy me a clarinet, and I spent a frustrating semester in Introductory Band, trying to learn how to blow through a clarinet reed amidst the din of beginning trumpets, oboes, bassoons, saxophones, and even a few drums.

I try to recall the moment when I finally decided to stop playing the violin. I suspect it took place in the interim before my father found a piano he wanted to buy, and that there was a nasty precipitating argument. A moment where he shouted at me and I threw down my instrument as tears washed my face, so that "deciding" misrepresents the desperate heat of my refusal. I hear myself complaining that I no longer enjoy practicing "one bit." "One doesn't practice for enjoyment," my father says, oblivious to the venomous glance I throw him. Perhaps I am even aggressive enough to answer that he himself rarely "practices": although he has a range of pieces he plays easily and must once have practiced with great dedication, he resists working through the difficult phrases of new compositions, as I am supposed to do. Sometimes, if he has made a mistake, when he comes to the end of the piece, he replays the section a couple of times before shrugging and pulling the cover down over the piano keys. I suspect that my father responds with equally pointed jabs, though his tone is mellow, bemused; and that the round continues with punches from each side, until I am like a wounded boxer, smarting, tipsy, aiming wildly. I suspect, too, that I go back on my decision, letting my father coax me into practicing once or twice, or even reluctantly agreeing that we should look for another teacher I might like better.

Still, our moments of musical union have ended. Easily distracted by his new job, my father moves quickly to a rage whose intimacy I am healthy enough to run from. At the same time, a budding sexuality, for which our émigré home has no room, has made me moody, irritable, and filled with inchoate longing.

When the grand piano my father had chosen finally arrived, my black violin case stood closed at its side. Sometimes when Barbara played her flute to my father's accompaniment, he lashed out at her mistakes, as he had at mine, until she was reduced to tears, unable to purse her lips for that careful blow, and, finally, shaking the miserable saliva from her mouthpiece, had to put away her flute in defeat. A year or so later, taking her cue from me, she too refused to go on, and her instrument lay in its narrow black case alongside mine. Like heroines who had thrown our pointed lances into the heart of the dragon, leaving it wounded in the dark forest, we relished our guilty victory.

IT IS CLEAR to me now that, despite all the time I spent as a child with my violin under my chin, sitting on the floor with pencils and paints, or doing deep knee bends against a ballet barre, my father never intended me to be an artist. Even the graduated sheets of drawing paper he handed out with such parsimony and discrimination were not meant to lead Barbara or me up the sure steps to Art. For each new picture, we were to start with rough yellow paper, moving to white only if our accomplishment merited a second draft, and finally, if the picture's theme and execution justified still better, we were allowed to try once again, this time on the large white exhibition-size sheets that had featured my skyscrapers and baseball stadium. What I mean is that all this artistic order was to give comfort to my father, surrounding him with a semblance of the romanticized standards of the world he had fled, even as it gave us the self-discipline to be accomplished and decorative wives. Art was the calling of others, extraordinary people who lived daring and abandoned lives, most especially men. I could take all the lessons that my father could afford, and no amount of hard work, gift, or passion would lead toward being an artist. For my father, there was a line between ordinary and extraordinary, a line which was not crossed by the accretions of effort, accomplishment, or deep feeling, but which remained there, absolute.

Unfortunately, even the library books and articles my father had urged on me brought their perils, as he himself was beginning to realize, too late. When as a teenager I was quarrelsome, contentious, sarcastic, or intellectually snotty, my father warned me that I was turning myself into a woman who would be unattractive to men—unmarriageable. James Joyce, according to him, had married a prostitute who never read a word he wrote. Though my father had wanted intellectual companionship enough to supply his oldest daughter with a stream of books, music, and art, he had nevertheless found this companionship more charming in a precocious child than in a prickly adolescent, who was unable to imagine a viable future.

ONE DAY IN high school, I was kicking pebbles as I poked along the far end of our hilly Seattle street. If I looked between the houses, I could glimpse the shimmering gray of Lake Washington a few streets below. Suddenly, the wail of an ambulance neared, and the white wagon raced by. Perhaps I sensed for a split second that some new tragedy could strike us. When I reached home, a neighbor was there to greet me: my father had had a heart attack, and my mother had accompanied him to the hospital.

I have no memory of the next days or weeks. I only know that when he was finally released from the hospital, our house was transformed. Miriam's mysterious difficulties had absorbed my mother's attention, leaving Barbara and me very much on our own. But now, as Miriam's panic at our father's frailty resulted in hysterical demands for care, Mother's attentions became divided, strained, often frantic. My father had been a sickly child in Vienna, and was an accustomed invalid. He cut back on patients and sank into an apathetic compliance to all healing routines: an austere diet (for some reason, mineral oil was now used to dress our salads), slow gentle walks, and absolute quiet for his daily rest. Even during those evening hours when he could be among the family, no one was allowed to upset him.

"Carol, watch your step!" Mother demanded, if I stopped by his chair with a question. When he summoned the interest to argue with me at the dinner table, Mother quickly interceded.

Was I starting those meal-time quarrels to draw my father out of his frightening despondency and retrieve our earlier companionship? His piles of half-read books seemed to grow, the emery boards stuck somewhere before the middle. Even with my vague understanding of the shape of careers, I sensed that he had changed direction too often, that in his restless moves from psychoanalysis through various schools of psychotherapy to behaviorism was a desperation that was unlikely to yield a creative synthesis, and that at some deep level perhaps unknown to him, he was giving up.

Yet sometimes my father would put away his library book and ask me to go for a walk. Then, as the pressure of his arm through our winter coats left me breathless with anxiety, I learned how judgment and passion ride on separate tracks. Our talks would be introspective, philosophical, rambling, and the sound of birds or a car passing seemed only to lock us further in our strange intimacy. I would be eager to tell him about the evils of capital punishment; my father, gloomy and reflective, would want to talk about a book he was reading. Or I would have discovered that Western dualism is the root of all misery; and my father would quote Catullus, or tell me to read Thomas Merton. Two dreamers roaming suburban streets together.

I was in college when on our long contemplative walks my father began to confide his discontent with my mother: she made it hard for him to discuss the issues he really cared about, and the slightest hint that he wanted something else from her reduced her to tears. Or he was feeling caught by being the steady breadwinner and wished that he hadn't ceded to her notions of a proper family life, which in America involved constant expenses. If only he had the freedom to experiment more in his work, but always caution—he saw how it was both internally and externally imposed—held him back. Breathless with the seriousness of his confession, I would silently vow never to curtail the creativity of the man I loved by making him support me and my children.

As we rounded the corner, in sight of our house, my face flushed with cold and excitement, I felt that I had gained some new stature, that I might even be protected against future humiliations. His arm dropped mine as we came up the walk. Once inside, my mother was irritable about some task I had left undone, and though I threw my father a wounded look, he was already behind a book or at his piano bench, in search of a score. I should have expected that no amount of shared confessions could win me special grace, and that nothing I had heard merited extra loyalty.

MY FATHER STILL owned his Austrian *Lederhosen* when he died, and, although he avoided buying all German and Austrian products and would not set foot on his homeland, he compared all American mountain ranges to the Alps. Perhaps that is why he chose to succumb in the Berkshires one August. It was his third heart attack, and I was a few days short of twenty-four.

The sight of my unused violin in its dark leather case by the piano had remained a perpetual reminder of my betrayal. Yet I seemed destined to cause him further disappointment—as well as to become accustomed to the lacerations of his criticisms. Uniformly unimpressed with the friends I brought home from school, my father's quickened interest once young men began to call quickly turned to searing judgment. I would tell him about a novel, a present from a young man I'd met, and my father would quickly find the time to read it—only to judge it poorly written and a superficial rendition of an old idea.

Still, my desire for my father's devotion was at least as tenacious as my blind struggle to increase my measure of autonomy. One day on a walk I pulled out a love letter I had received, and I believe that not even my father, with his psychoanalytic sophistication, questioned either my doing this or his interest in reading it. No, this sharing seemed appropriate to, an integral part of, our intimacy. Carefully, he read both sides of the page as I awaited his judgment with a hot face; then, returning the precious sheet, he reported that the letter worried him as the young man seemed shallow, vain, and potentially cruel.

The January before I graduated from college, I began to live with an ambitious scholarship student from a tumultuous Jewish working-class family. The young man's bookcases were detailed testimony to the influences and interests he was acquiring through voracious reading, as he set his sights on entering the pantheon of great writers. While his nervous energies were entirely focused on this future he was crafting, he seemed more able to accommodate a girlfriend with intellectual and artistic inclinations than my father had been able to tolerate them in a daughter. Although my father had only shown scorn for conventional morality, both in letters and face-to-face he pronounced my live-in arrangement as masochistic and uncontrolled: I had defiled myself, he argued, and was wasting my life.

In his conviction that I was headed down a path of abuse with men, was my father viewing me through the gendered myths of his profession, or narcissistically seeing himself mirrored in my choices? And would he have viewed it as the break it would some-day be, had I brought home a potential partner who was reliable, kind and warm?

The final rift came when I returned in late winter from a year in Spain and Morocco with hepatitis, and without the insurance to pay for hospitalization or doctors. Worse, the young man, who was now my legal husband, had excused himself from any conventional obligations, and, irrespective of my medical needs, was planning to

continue writing the novel he had started abroad. Absolving himself of all economic responsibility for my situation, my father emphasized the rupture by also ceasing all communication with me. I
don't even know if he was aware that I managed to get myself admitted to a hospital ward for medically indigent patients, where I
spent the next five weeks in bed, surrounded by a range of lively
Spanish voices. (Hepatitis, even without a family crisis, is accompanied by a clinical depression, but my gloom was regularly inter-
rupted by using the language I had learned in Spain to explain to the
woman in the next bed that it was her kidney troubling her, or to
translate the doctor's directives.) Several months later, still weak
from hepatitis, I took the Greyhound bus from New York to Washington, D.C., for Barbara's June wedding. Throughout the ceremony
and subsequent garden party, my father maintained his stony silence, turning his head whenever I looked at him, and charming the
lowliest of guests to avoid talking to me.

He had still made no attempt to write or speak to me when in August I got a long-distance phone call to come and help bury him in
New Hampshire, in the mountainous landscape he loved.

THERE IS A black-and-white photograph of my father and me in
profile, playing music together. The photographer must have
crouched on the stairs behind the banister of our Topeka house, for
the picture cuts us at our waists. My straight brown hair is parted on
the side and held back in a plastic clip. With my soft round cheeks
and small high nose, I look sweetly innocent, unscarred. I am surprised at what a pretty girl I was – something I was never told.
(What I was told, by my mother, was that I didn't look Jewish, which
seemed to cause her both sorrow and guilty relief.) My father sits
bent toward the piano, his shoulders sloped inside one of the
woolen shirts he continued to wear, always fearing a chill, even after
the women in the family had switched to spring clothes. An unruly
strand of dark hair hangs over his furrowed forehead. I imagine that

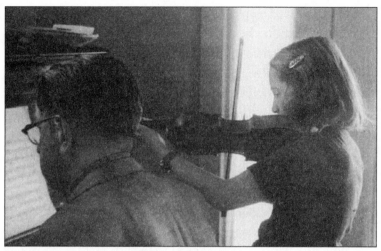

My father accompanying me on the violin. My bad posture must have contributed to the aches that plagued me as long as I practiced.

he is humming along in his na-na-na tuneless way, as if he felt the need to be a human metronome, or thought he was augmenting the melody, thickening the texture of the composition.

Who took the picture? I was the first in the family to own a camera, a "Baby Brownie Special," which I bought with my allowance when I was ten. But this is a professional photograph, probably taken by my Uncle Manfred, who would have been proud to capture the romance in the scene.

NEARLY A DECADE after my father's death, I was leaving my apartment to move in with an undisciplined charismatic man who, I already knew, would be unreliable and unfaithful, and whose pervasive contempt took the form of saying whatever was expedient, no matter how it strayed from the truth. This last was a new twist in torture for me. Words had often been cruel, but they had always referred to something I could follow. Though I already did not like this man, and probably knew I would one day have to leave him, I was in love with him.

All these years, I had taken my violin wherever I went. At Vassar, I had played in the orchestra. But practicing alone in the dusty conservatory rooms, so cut off from the rest of the campus, made my shoulder ache in bitterness, loneliness, and sorrow. Still, I sometimes opened my violin case over the next years, rosined my bow and played awhile, in the faint hope that I might find a way to retrieve my connection to music, beyond the grip of my father. Now I had put all my effects in boxes, in preparation for the move. And then I began taking everything down to the U-Haul van. Books, a smattering of furniture, prints and posters, worn suitcases filled with clothes. I was still living like a student. As I went in and out of my apartment, I glimpsed my violin standing upright in its black case, like an old cat waiting to see if it would be taken along. And then came the moment when I closed the door for the last time, knowing that my violin stood there, abandoned.

11

City of Grief

6

In *Deutsch*

IT IS SPRING 1995 WHEN I NERVOUSLY stand in line in a large wide-windowed room of New York University's Deutsches Haus, around the corner from my office. Having recently won a fellowship from the Memorial Foundation for Jewish Culture to investigate my father's Viennese career, including his time as a psychoanalytic pedagogue, whose brief history is little known, I am at Deutsches Haus to take a placement test for an intensive summer course in German. Although the fellowship will lessen the financial strain of spending the coming October in Vienna, its real value, as I already suspect, is to throw a cloak of scholarly investigation over my tangled emotions.

I am shaking as the woman in front of me goes before the tribunal of German teachers sitting behind the long pine table. Her crisp confident English carries in the silence of the large sunny room where other prospective students sit at solitary desk-chairs, obediently completing their placement tests. Like me, this woman has received a grant and plans to work in German-language archives. But her voice cascades toward the high ceiling as she insists that she has no use for a conversation course, and she pushes away the placement test that the Deutsches Haus teacher tries to hand her; she would rather be challenged, she says, than bored.

When I finally face the German teacher, like someone with a bad conscience, I meekly accept my exam. Two pages of German sentences contain blanks that call for the nominative, accusative, and dative forms of pronouns. Though the answers come quickly, my hand trembles as I fill them in. When I last took a test, the comprehensive exams for my Ph.D., was I this afraid?

No, something about my project—about *Deutsch*, about my father—has provoked this archaic fear. Though I am eager to spend time in Vienna, I am also afraid of the dark pit of wounded love around which I have carefully walked for so many years. Back at the pine table, where the German teacher has quickly corrected my exam, a giggle rises in my throat, part terror, part relief, when she points to a couple of mistakes and instructs me in German to sign up for the advanced class. Tongue-tied, I finally respond to her in English, feeling a shameful familiarity in our "bilingual" conversation, as if I am again the breakaway child, neither European nor quite American.

That evening, with German once again in my inner ear, I suddenly think of myself as an amputee. Although I have taken the first step to get my limb back, I find myself wanting, and not wanting, the language and connections I've done without since my father's death.

THE REALIZATION THAT I knew so little about my father's Viennese past—and could actually know more, without much difficulty—had come several months earlier. There were simple things, like the old photographs from Vienna I had found by chance in a frayed brown envelope at the bottom of my mother's buffet, and had never really looked at. I remembered the unopened folder of his American articles, which his research assistant at the National Institute of Mental Health had sent me shortly after he died. And I knew the addresses of a handful of former friends and colleagues, some of them Viennese, even if I wasn't in touch with them.

From one day to the next, my ignorance became unacceptable. Nevertheless, wanting to learn about his early life in Vienna, or to read the intellectual work he had produced in America, embarrassed me with its unresolved passion. My own two careers, as a writer and an anthropologist who studied urban schools, had moved fitfully, in part because of my split efforts. Still more hampering was a self-effacing streak that made me miss or botch opportunities. Yet I was happy in a second marriage, and had belatedly taken a full-time research position in a recently opened multiracial policy institute at New York University. Since the research was engaging, and I was working with a lively group of committed colleagues, why was I suddenly going to take time out to uncover who, other than my father, Paul Bergmann had been?

WALKING HOME FROM German class in the warm evenings, I wondered about the language of my infancy. My parents spoke German to each other and to my grandmother Antonie, but how much German did I speak as a child? *"Meine Lieblingssprache,"* a classmate, Berthe, called it. A portly vivacious woman with ruddy skin and coarse bleached hair, Berthe's German was from Leipzig, where she had lived until the age of ten. *Lieblingssprache*—the word was new to me. I translated it as a favorite language, or a language of love, or even the language in which one has been loved. But *Liebling* is a term of endearment, like darling; as with so many German words, it felt more evocative than any English translation.

On the streets of New York I sometimes overheard Berthe's *Lieblingssprache* in the quiet confiding tones of Jewish refugees. Now in their eighties and nineties, their effort to hold their backs straight under the weight of their old coats was palpable, as they walked arm in arm. While the elderly German Jews made me feel the grieving stone that always lies between my breasts, the German of young tourists, stopping on a street corner to consult their maps, sounded abrupt, arrogant, too loud. It provoked in me an explosive fearful rage—"How dare you speak that language here!"—that made me unable to reach out in *Deutsch* to help them find their way.

And was German my *Lieblingssprache*—child of the Kansas plains that I was?

What I remembered was the isolating cocoon of German in our house on Lindenwood, and the intimacy of sitting with my father at the piano, as we sang the lieder of Schubert or Hugo Wolf.

But I could also hear my mother impatiently reprimand Grandmother Antonie, "*Mutti*, speak English, we're in America now," as if it were a question of my grandmother, who had never studied English, making up her mind to try harder.

And I heard myself pleading, "Mother, when my friends come over, please don't speak German!" Which, of course, suggested that she had talked to me in German, not only when I was home alone, but when other children were in the house.

Beginning to think in *Deutsch* after so many years brought a lush warm joy, but also insecurity and shame whenever I heard my own mistakes. Despite the German classics that grounded our bookcases and my father's intellect, my German had remained peculiarly illiterate. Only in college had I belatedly received the elementary rules of grammar and spelling that any third or fourth grader learns in school. Besides, it had been decades since those brief college years. Though I had become my father's high-achieving daughter, German exposed the raw gap between my skill and the standards by which he would have judged me. The *Deutsch* I needed to speak was fluent, literate, without an accent; but my vocabulary was a primitive net filled with holes, my grammar could falter, and my r's were the sharp flat r's of the American Midwest.

I HAD SPENT ten hot days in Vienna the August I turned twenty-eight. It was four years after my father's sudden death, and two months after my young husband had left me for the erotic adventures that he belatedly believed were necessary to becoming an important American writer. In open sandals I wandered the dense, elegant, curving streets of the Inner City, Vienna's First District, and followed the wide grassy boulevards of the Ringstrasse. In my wallet lay the slip of paper on which my mother had written my father's Viennese address, but day after day I couldn't even take the paper out. I let myself be picked up by a thin Syrian engineering student, who moved me from my pension into his sparsely furnished apartment in the immigrant quarter on the far side of the Danube. "A young woman should not stay by herself in a strange city," he said sadly, as if to minimize his confusion at defiling an American stranger; but the Arabic that shaped his unassuming German comforted me.

Everything about Vienna seemed overwhelming and sinister to me that sweltering August of 1969: the immense Baroque-style public edifices grandly spaced along the Ring; the well-dressed couples, just the age to have been Nazis, sitting over coffee and beautiful cakes in outdoor cafés; the high-steepled Stefanskirche, whose clerics had stirred hatred against Jews. Even the Viennese pronunciation I recognized from my father sounded narrow-minded and cruel.

One day as my feet burned from the pavement, a red haze colored the air before my eyes. Why was I, abandoned by my boy-husband to whom I had clung in the wake of my father's terrible death, stranded in this city where he himself had refused to return? *Wien*, city of loss, city of grief! Finally, having never taken his address out of my wallet, I left impulsively on an afternoon train.

AS IT HAPPENED, my research stay in Vienna began on the afternoon before Yom Kippur, the Day of Atonement. In New York, I had envisioned spending my first evening in the Stadttempel, Vienna's main synagogue. I had even promised my Aunt Edith, who at ninety was active in her Conservative synagogue and coaxing me toward observance, that I would begin my October in that still famously antisemitic city by joining in the fasting and prayers of Jews' most sacred holiday. As usual, imagining myself immersed in a Jewish ritual brought a certain comfort, even pride.

But I didn't go to the great Stadttempel on Seitenstättengasse (or to any other synagogue) that first evening. Instead, I busied myself with unpacking and arranging my clothing and papers in the vast, cluttered, book-lined room that had been a conservatory in better days, when my landlady was still married to a famous violinist. A sitting area by the door looked onto a grand piano, behind which crouched my narrow studio bed, along with an armoire and a small roll-top desk. Yet if my landlady had decided to make a profit from the once-elegant room, she had cleared no space for a lodger; even the armoire was too crammed to use. After poking about, I hung my few blouses and pairs of slacks on a mahogany valet that had probably held the violinist's tuxedoes. It was after eight when I finally felt sufficiently settled to venture out, and I only went as far as an Indian restaurant, a few doors away.

The next morning, Yom Kippur, I didn't leave early for services, being careful not to swallow water when I brushed my teeth, but drank my hot coffee with an excellent dark roll that I purchased with relish in a tiny but excellent bakery across the street. My landlady would be in Buenos Aires for the first three weeks of my stay, but she had left me a set of "temporary residence" forms, along with a note that I had forty-eight hours to turn them in. So I walked across Beatrixgasse to the nearest police station to present my completed forms, before beginning my first day of research, as if it were an ordinary day—except that, as always on the High Holidays, I felt nervous and out of sorts, and measured the hours by the progress of the ritual I was missing. How I longed to hear the haunting melody of the *Amidah*, the song of devotion and faith, and the rumbling of the congregation saying *Yizkor*, the prayer for the dead. In synagogue, I would have thought of my father and grandfather and all the other relatives whose names I didn't even know who had lived and died in this city—just as I thought of them now, in my self-imposed exile. With sundown came the beautiful *Na'ila* service I was missing, and I watched along with those at prayer for the first star, marking the formal end of the day. The knowledge that Vienna's Jews were finally streaming out of the synagogue to end their long fast brought me my own peculiar relief.

AS LONG AS I lived with my parents, both Vienna and Berlin lay on the dark side of a dreaded gravitational field that held me captive, neither free to escape, nor able to reach back and make contact. Though memories of internment, hiding and escape, death and wandering, had threaded adult conversation in our house, my child's sense of this history was fragmentary and uncertain. As with a great passion that has ended in betrayal, or a tragic unrequited love, the humiliation, anger and longing of my parents' dashed futures, of having been hated and "kicked out" (my mother's words), had been passed onto me, where they lodged between my shoulders and tightened my gait.

Still, amidst the *Heimweh* that hung over our household, I had drawn one lesson: passivity was dangerous, and even if survival were a matter of luck, vigilance and will brought the only chances for saving oneself. Which was why, soon after we moved east to Bethesda, Barbara and I had arrived at the wild hope that we could do something. From baby-sitting and other stray jobs, our pooled savings came to several hundred hard-earned dollars. Although our enthusiasms rarely coincided, in a marvelous juncture of cascading agreement, we had decided that Mother and Father should return to visit their native cities. This, perhaps exactly this, would bring relief to our refugee home, freeing us at last from dislocation and sorrow.

At the travel agency we discovered that Vienna was quite far from Berlin, and that flights to either city were more expensive than the more commonly advertised destinations—Paris, London, Frankfurt. (Like the paltry European geography of our classmates, ours was incredibly vague.) Finally, in an unlikely compromise, we purchased two tickets to Frankfurt, the least expensive European destination. From there Mother and Father could take a train to either of their homes. I began to imagine them like the well-dressed diplomats in newsreels, victoriously waving as they emerged from the plane door onto a red-carpeted stairway.

In a dither of suspense, we sat Mother and Father down on the living room couch for the presentation of their gift. But as soon as they removed the tickets from the envelope, I saw the severity of our mistake.

"That's very generous." Mother's face was drawn and her lips tight. "But don't you two have anything better to do with your money?"

"We really want you to go to Vienna and Berlin!"

"I am happy to visit Berlin, Maryland, which will save you a lot of money," said Father, not even looking at us. Berlin was a tiny hamlet that had whizzed by, causing much amusement, as we drove from Bethesda to the Atlantic Ocean.

"Daddy!" My voice rang with despair.

"I have no interest in visiting either Germany or Austria." This time his point came frontally. "Perhaps your mother wants to go alone."

Mother shook her head.

"Oh Daddy, just for a vacation!" Barbara cried out.

He slipped the tickets back into their envelope. "I assume they're refundable," he said, getting up.

A BRICK FACADE across the street from Vienna's Third District police station off Landstrasse, a number of blocks from the Inner City, advised, "*Rassismus ist kein Spass,*" Racism is no joke. The poster suggested two lines of thought: that casual acts of racism were more than a marginal problem in Vienna, and that racism was not acceptable, at least among some Viennese.

The precinct station was barricaded by construction scaffolding, but a sign directed those with residence registration forms to a side door under the dark passageway. The precinct station near my apartment, where I had gone the previous morning, had advised me that only this station handled the residence forms of foreign visitors. Now I was nearing the end of the legal period for registering myself.

In the small steamy waiting room of the station, Turks worked their worry beads as they talked quietly. Bosnians and Croatians in worn leather jackets gathered in clumps to compare their forms and give each other helpful hints. An Indian woman, a heavy gray sweater subduing her colorful sari, found in a fellow countryman the expertise to help translate the bureaucratic German as she waited her turn. This was the "multicultural society" about which Jörg Haider and his Freedom Party were stirring up their fellow Austrians; *"Wien soll nicht Chicago werden!"* Don't let Vienna become Chicago! one of the many Haider posters around the city warned. Compared to either Chicago or my New York, Vienna seemed homogeneous, sedate, and strikingly Caucasian—not that different from when Hitler had decried it as a *"Rassenbabylon,"* a racial Babylon, and accused its citizens of "scandalous miscegenation." Yet Bosnian and Croatian refugees had nearly doubled the number of foreigners (from 5.3 to 9 percent) between 1990 and 1995, and several letter bombs had been aimed at Austria's minorities, as well as at public figures working with refugees.

Across from the waiting room entrance was a closed inner door on which a hand-printed sign warned in German, "Do not knock. Take a number. You will be called in turn." But since the automatic number dispenser was not working—as each newcomer discovered, giving it a hard useless punch—the foreigners crammed in the hot room were quietly showing each new person whom to follow.

Every few minutes the internal door opened briefly, as someone exited from the interview and gave those still waiting a comradely nod. Then, as the next person rose to enter the inner office, I could hear the sharp nasal interrogators behind the door. That bored, impatient, insinuating tone, which I had already experienced at the service windows of the post office and the train station, didn't ease my anticipation of my interview—especially since I was mortified about how I had filled out my form.

It was *Religionsbekenntnis* that had been my downfall. Literally translated, the word asked which religion I "confessed" or "owned up" to.

The fact was, the Austrian authorities were uninterested in my meta-physical ruminations, and I had not owned up to the heritage that had brought me to my father's city. Instead, being in Vienna had evoked childhood anxieties that I thought had disappeared during my three decades in New York. There had been the probably harmless detail of a dissonance between the top sheet of the form, which contained the *Religionsbekenntnis* question, and the copies which didn't. "Bud-dhist," I had scribbled, my heart pounding. My outlandish and cow-ardly answer reminded me of our Unitarian neighbors in Seattle, whom my mother had referred to with distaste as "Jews in hiding," and put into question the sturdy integrity I had assumed would carry me through five weeks alone in Vienna.

Looking around the room, I imagined the Turkish man with the worry beads answering "Lutheran" on his form. After all, he was a more visible target than I in the *Rassenbabylon* of contemporary Vi-enna. (This was long before the bombing of the World Trade Center had given Muslim men a justifiable fear of being considered terror-ists, and so a reason to imagine self-disguise.) Was I still held so cap-tive by the Nazi stories of my childhood, or the petty American antisemitism of the 1950s that had prompted Jewish movie stars to change their names and our neighbors to choose an easier religious identity? Taking out my pen, I was ready to cross out Buddhist, or even redo the entire form. Should I answer, "*Hebraisch*" or "*Israëlitis-che*," as was the customary designation for Jews in contemporary Austria? "*Jude*" was another possibility, as was recreating the thick one-inch high "J" that during the Third Reich had been stamped on all official documents of Jews. The thought rode on a wave of bel-ligerence that was a flimsy mask for the terror I couldn't subdue.

The door opened as a man came out; it was suddenly my turn. Fumbling to put my pen back in my purse, I hurried into the inter-rogation room.

"*Grüss Gott*," I mimicked the Austrian greeting with nervous cheer.

The woman behind the desk gave me an irritated glance as she turned over my form, making sure I had answered all the questions, and stamped each of the three copies. Then, tearing off the first copy on which I had written that I was a Buddhist, she placed it on her stack and gave me back the other two. Reminding me that I had to submit a copy to the police station before I left Vienna to return to New York, she motioned me out of the room.

I was now a legal resident of my father's city, and the official count of Viennese Buddhists had just increased by one. But in my uneasiness and suspicion, I felt very much a Jew.

Werdertorgasse

ALONE WITH MY OWN INTERNAL mooring, the borders between present and past were porous, easily dissolved. Though I felt surrounded by an ancient and timeless city, a mobile museum parked near my apartment, next to the Landstrasse open-air market, brought me up short with its photographic exhibition of Vienna's devastation by Allied bombs and the vast rebuilding efforts after 1945. Much of the city directly around me was actually new since the war. Memories of my Topeka childhood alternated with imagined scenes from my father's *Wien*. Any street sign, poster, advertisement, or bit of news seemed to cause the mental slippage, re-hinging my thoughts onto one of these several pasts. Although the pale October sun disappeared in sudden darkness around five, and I was systematically marking off each day with accomplished tasks, I seemed to be living outside chronology.

One day, I misread a *Sonderangebot*—special sale—notice papered on a store window as *Sonderkommando*, the special squads of Jews forced to feed the gas chambers and crematoria with the corpses of their own people. Transforming an innocent prompt to consumerism into the darkest moments of the Third Reich seemed a ridiculous mistake. But it made me suspect that, in searching to uncover the story my father had deliberately kept to himself, I must feel I was veering toward terrible disloyalty.

With my landlady away, my only companion was a skinny violin student, a young Jew from Moscow, who rented another room in the once grand apartment. Yuri's straight dark hair fell into his boyish face when he wasn't wearing a baseball cap backward, American style. Having grown up under the Soviet system, he knew little about Jewish religious practice; but he advertised his heritage with a gold Star of David that hung below the Adam's apple of his thin neck, and he was bumptious and mistrustful of the Viennese, whom he assumed to be antisemitic.

During my first days in Vienna, Yuri had acted as my rushed host, pausing on his way out, his violin case hanging at his knees, to offer me tips—a monthly pass that would enable me to use any streetcar or underground; an inexpensive Indian restaurant nearby; concerts for which there were special tickets—and our common Jewish heritage gave us a tenuous link. But Yuri's elaborate courtships kept him out until early morning, and he slept into the afternoon, when he emerged smelling of men's lotions—late, always late!—to dash out for classes at the Vienna Conservatory.

When our paths did cross, our conversations were increasingly focused on the house telephone. It had been plugged into a jack in the hall when I arrived; and I thought it should be kept there, available to us both. But, except when he was leaving for a long evening and graciously installed the phone in my room, along with a notepad so that I could act as his social secretary, Yuri kept locking it inside his room. How the sound of the ringing phone behind his door—which might well be my husband Bob with a comforting call from New York—made me grit my teeth!

Three times a week, I ended my day in a once-elegant building across the street from the open-air stalls of the *Naschmarkt*. Like a character in *The Third Man*, I pulled the elevator switch and, from inside a beautiful hand-operated glass-cage, watched the floors recede beneath me. A short greeting with the orange-clothed swami at the registration table was often my most intimate exchange of the day. (Was it merely the familiar *Du* used at the Yoga Center, when all my other encounters were *Sie*?) Changing into loose clothes, I entered the empty white room whose broad windows looked far down onto the piles of fruit and vegetables, fresh bread and cheese, tended by Vienna's Middle Eastern immigrants. Then, along with a dozen Viennese, I gave myself to that hour-and-a-half of focused timelessness that constitutes yoga. How much more powerful the teacher's instructions seemed in German! *"Beine locker lassen"* meant nothing more than "relax your legs," which I heard regularly in New York, but issued in *Deutsch,* the instructions turned me into a child again, and I succumbed to their primitive power.

Although my Viennese days were structured by the schedule I had constructed of necessary archival visits, in the interstices of yoga, or sitting before records at a library table, my thoughts roamed back in time to the man who had been my father. What had made him so angry? What I meant by this was the bitterness that had kept him from returning to his native city, as well as his sudden rage at me or my sisters and his irritability with my mother. In the early wake of his death, I had minimized his refusal to speak to me during his last six months, including through my long illness. It was an aberration, I told myself; what I would hold onto were the many interests we had shared, the times we had understood each other instinctively, and the ways I had become like him. But his last silence had become more punishing over the years. Sometimes I wondered if I hadn't come to Vienna as a last desperate effort to trick him into speaking. Had he been as angry here, as a young man? Or had his forced emigration changed him into the brooding, easily enraged husband and father who had made life so treacherous for the women in our family? Actually, I had a clue: others in my extended family, even those who had survived concentration camps, had emerged from the Nazi years with their good spirits a bit crispy but intact. Something about his first thirty-three years in Vienna, about his makeup and his family and the city he had loved and grown to hate, had formed the charming, often cruel father I knew and still missed—and for whom I needed to finish grieving.

When the elegant aristocratic palaces of the Inner City reminded me of Topeka's simple two-story wooden houses with their wide front porches, I felt my father's alienation in that small midwestern town, where even the State Capitol seemed an innocent and playful imitation of architectural stature. No wonder he hadn't wanted to see his beautiful lost city again! Sometimes, too, as I hopped onto the Ring-Kai-Ring streetcar that circled the Inner City, I was reminded that we in America had never agreed to civilize our cities: while Vienna spread like a jeweled necklace along the Danube, its majestic public buildings connected to one another by street cars running promptly along well-designed boulevards, the cities of the United States were unclaimed orphans, daily destroyed and rebuilt with indifference, their natural topographies disguised by weedy skyscrapers, and their fragile neighborhoods split open by overpasses and highways on which people drove in their lonely air-conditioned cars.

Yet, as in yoga, my dreamlike state during those long solitary Viennese days often overflowed with happiness at being surrounded by Vienna's idiosyncratic German, which reunited me with the melodic sounds of my father. And I was overcome with euphoria as I imagined him moving about his splendid quirky city, as I was learning to do. Was I asking myself about his anger, then, to contain my surges of old love? Perhaps. Like the sun of October, however, even my moments of happiness were threaded with a melancholy chill. Turning a corner, I might feel close to glimpsing my father— might even see his beloved shadow at the edge of my vision. Sometimes, too, opening an archival file, I almost heard his curious warm voice. Yet in the end his silence remained absolute, and I knew nothing could bring him back. Indeed, with every passing hour, his death of thirty years was receding further into a dimming past.

I HAD WRITTEN the archivist at the Israëlitische Kultusgemeinde that I intended to pay a visit. In the nineteenth century, when the vital statistics of most Viennese were kept by the Catholic Church, Emperor Franz Josef created this Jewish civic and cultural organization attached to the Stadttempel, Vienna's main synagogue, to house the records of the city's Jews. However, to give the appearance of an all-Catholic empire, only Catholic churches were allowed to use identifiable religious architecture, and the complex on Seittenstättengasse, a short narrow pedestrian street a few blocks from the Danube Canal, remains indistinguishable from an ordinary residential or office building. Nevertheless, the address is well known to Austrians and others, who periodically threaten the building. In addition to a soldier with a machine gun who paces the narrow street, two German-speaking Israelis sit in a guardroom just inside the heavy windowless front door.

My fellowship award letter from the Memorial Foundation for Jewish Culture would have been the obvious solution to the guards' demand for proof of my purpose, but I was finding it unexpectedly hard to claim my roots in Vienna, and I hadn't brought the letter along.

"*Sie sind Jude?*" the young Israeli demanded roughly. You're a Jew?

"*Ja, natürlich!*" I said, irrationally insulted by his question.

"What synagogue do you attend?"

Aghast at having to prove myself in the one Viennese institution to which I surely had rights, my mind jammed. In New York, I would have comfortably admitted that I wasn't a member of any synagogue. Here, my blood raced as I blurted a garbled version of an Upper West Side synagogue where I had stood several times in the back aisle alongside other "Yom Kippur Jews" who didn't plan sufficiently ahead to obtain a spot on the wooden benches. The guard snorted. I thought he might ask me to recite the *Sh'ma*. Instead he barked at me to open my bag. Having unzipped it for his inspection, I watched him pull out my camera and threaten to expose the film.

Finally, he pressed a button, and I moved inside the first of two electronic doors. There I remained, imprisoned between sheets of soundproof glass, watching the guards' mouths move in comradely chatter. I had been brought up to believe that we Jews ensured our own safety, not by walling ourselves off from others, but by creating a just and tolerant world. This universalistic ethic, which my parents had shared despite their temperamental differences, was why in the late 1930s they had each resisted emigration to what was then Palestine. Although the promise of safety based on tolerance and equality may prove to be a kind of secular faith, I had absorbed it into my own system of reason and was taken aback whenever Jews drew from the Holocaust an entirely different lesson: the urgency to protect ourselves against a hostile world, irrespective of the moral price.

The second glass door slid open, and quickly shut behind me again. I stood locked inside the synagogue compound.

I had expected a Jewish institution to be a haven of comfort in Vienna. I might choose to stand as an observer in the back aisle, but as in the Upper West Side synagogue I would soak in the reflected comfort of community. Yet, if the encounter at the police station had awakened fears of my Jewish identity, the heavily guarded insularity of Judaism at the Kultusgemeinde made me feel trapped inside someone else's ghetto.

In the early decades of the twentieth century, my father and his parents were among the 175,000 Viennese Jews, constituting a sizeable twenty percent of Vienna's inhabitants. Though Jews were barred from important civic positions, Vienna was a city where Jews could succeed, and the emperor was generally considered a friend of Jews. At the end of World War I, when the defeated Habsburg Empire was divided into autonomous countries, Jews played important political roles in the First Austrian Republic, and particularly in Vienna's socialist city government. While the Christian Fascist regime installed after the Civil War of 1934 brought growing difficulties for Jews, it was only after the *Anschluss* in 1938, when Adolf Eichmann was put in charge of solving Austria's "Jewish problem" that Vienna quickly became a model of forced emigration. By November 1941, just after my grandmother was finally able to leave, only 44,000 Jews

remained in the city, and Eichmann's assignment switched from fa-
cilitating emigration to expediting deportation to Theresienstadt
and other concentration camps of the Third Reich. Over the next
four years, 38,000 Viennese Jews were sent to concentration camps,
where most were murdered by starvation and gassing. In 1945, only
6,000 Jews remained in Vienna—nearly all had been protected by
conversion and marriage to Aryans. Soon these survivors were joined
by another 5,000 Polish, Czech, Hungarian, and Russian Jews making their way out of the concentration camps.[1] Since the 1980s, this
small group has been augmented by Jewish immigrants from the
former Soviet Union (among them my housemate Yuri), as well as
from Israel, Hungary, and other former Eastern bloc countries, bringing Vienna's Jewish population to between 20,000 and 30,000. Nevertheless, most Jews in 1995 appeared to resist association with a
Jewish organization, and the Israëlitische Kultusgemeinde counted
a mere 7,800 members.[2]

The archive was located at the end of a narrow hall. A dim light
that in the United States would denote "closed" was barely visible
through a smoky glass door on which a sign read, "Those seeking
family information may come on Monday—Thursday afternoon,
or by appointment." It was Thursday, but not yet afternoon. I
knocked timidly, waited, then knocked a little harder.

The door was opened by a harried middle-aged woman whose
tense face was fringed by short dark hair. A tan cardigan drawn over
a plain cotton dress, and the slippers favored by Central European
cleaning women, made me wonder if she were there to sweep.
Barely nodding, she turned back into the small room and disappeared down a few stairs into an adjoining office. The room where
I stood was windowless and shabby. Behind a large heavy wooden
table, enormous leather-bound books stood upright on old shelves.
I set down my knapsack, opened my notebook, and laid my pen and
dictionary on the table. When after a few minutes neither the
woman nor anyone else had appeared, I stood at the steps to the
inner office.

"Excuse me, I wrote some time ago about wanting to look for information on Paul Bergmann," I announced in German, taking out my business card.

"*Ach*, I wondered when that woman from New York would come." Reluctantly, she stood up from her desk.

"Are you the archivist, Frau Heidi Weiss?"

She nodded, her open slippers slapping the steps as she came towards me.

I wanted to start with learning about my father's birth; but I suddenly wasn't sure whether he had been born in 1905 or 1906. The set of large, heavy, leather-bound *Geburtsbuch*, or birth books, was chronological. Frau Weiss pulled down the 1905 book, which was structured like an accounting ledger. Each birth was recorded by hand beneath the previous entry, with other pertinent information concerning the infant's family and the circumstances of the birth filling columns across both sides of the open book. Since Paul was born at the end of January, I quickly saw that he wasn't there.

Frau Weiss had pulled down the next huge volume, when, several pages in, I caught my father's name at the top of the page.

Paul Bergmann born 29 January 1906, on Grünenthorgasse 19, in the 9th District.

My mother's slip of paper had read Werdertorgasse, in the Inner City, and I had assumed that he had always lived there. Moving across the page, I saw that Eduard Bergmann, my grandfather, had been born in Drevikov in Bohemia in 1872, but that Antonie Rotholz, my grandmother, was a native Viennese. (Her newly widowed mother and six older brothers—Jakob, Emanuel, Philipp, Ignatz, Karl, and Max—as I would discover, had come to Vienna from Sceznice, a village in Moravia, to work as peddlers shortly before her birth in 1880.) Another column listed Paul's four grandparents, whom I had never heard of. One of the grandmothers had even attended the registration, signing the book "Sophie Mahler

Bergmann" in her own steady round hand. So she was the source of Paul's relationship to the composer Gustav Mahler. Then came the name of the midwife, as well as the *mohel* who had performed the ritual circumcision.

"Magyarfalu—in 1903, that would have been a very romantic place to get married," Frau Weiss volunteered, her forefinger, with its cracked pink nail polish, directing my eye across the page.

"Where is it?"

"A couple of hours from Vienna." Shuffling over to a map on the wall of her inner office, she pointed out a small mountain resort, famous for its large ornate synagogue when my grandparents were getting married.

Though I had seen a photograph of my grandmother as a strong, dark-haired young woman wearing a large hat set at a tilt and long white suit, it had never occurred to me that this might be her wedding picture. Perhaps her proud brothers had treated her to the photograph to commemorate her marriage. A parallel photo by the same photographer showed Eduard. I knew from my father's cousin, now living in Australia, that Antonie's brother Max had turned his peddler's wagon into a successful second-hand linen and carpet business, and that he and his brothers had contributed to Antonie's dowry. But I didn't know why Eduard had been considered worth the dowry, and I had never considered how growing up in a fatherless family alongside five brothers might have shaped either my grandmother's wedding plans or her ideas about how a husband and wife could partner in marriage.

Since Frau Weiss had said that the records in the Kultusgemeinde concerned only births and deaths, I jumped forward nearly forty years to the one Viennese death I knew about, my grandfather Eduard's. In late 1940, Paul, who was in Hawaii, had sent his parents tickets to get out of Vienna, following the eastern route my other grandparents had taken, across Russia to Japan. It was Eduard's sudden death, just before the United States declared war on Japan, which delayed Antonie's parting and almost prevented her escape.

Down in her office, Frau Weiss went to a wooden cupboard of small drawers, from which she pulled out an index card for Eduard Bergmann. Silently jotting down the information, she handed me a scrap of paper.

"Died 10 December 1940. Kolschitzkygasse. Heart failure."

"May I please see the card?" I asked.

For a moment, I was disoriented. Werdertorgasse had been my one fact about my father's Viennese home. But the street was still another new address.

"This isn't the street where he lived," I said shakily.

"*Na ja*, in this period all Jews were forced out of their own homes into *Gruppenwohnungen*, group homes," Frau Weiss explained wearily. How often she must have repeated such painful facts to naïve Americans and Israelis who had come with the optimistic task of discovering their roots. She studied the card. "Kolschitzky-gasse, it's near the train station, one of those addresses."

My eyes blurred as I imagined my grandfather's life ending, not in his own home of thirty years, but crowded into a strange apartment along with other Jews being readied for deportation. Heart failure. A man of sixty-eight, wondering what new trial he and his wife would face at the hands of the Nazis. Perhaps the tickets had arrived when he could no longer muster the hope necessary for emigration. Had my grandfather passed on his expressive heart to my father?

"What does 'heart failure' mean?" I asked irritably, thinking of both Eduard's and my father's death.

"*Na ja*, it could be, in those terrible times a lot of Jews died by their own hands. But of course our records wouldn't show that."

The awful possibility took my breath away. Why had that never occurred to me? I had read that the Nazis' vicious household searches, particularly in the homes of the elderly, were often fol-lowed by suicides. Which made the tact of the Kultusgemeinde all the more poignant. Jewish law forbids taking one's own life. But

Jewish history was littered with pogroms long before Hitler, and Jewish institutions have learned to accommodate dark times. The note card gave a plot number in the Zentralfriedhof, the large cemetery at the southern outskirts of Vienna. My grandfather had lain there for fifty-five years without a visitor. Suddenly I was angry at my father. He had always spoken so warmly of his father. Could hatred of a country be so overwhelming as to prevent one from visiting a parent's grave? Or was this simply my father the rationalist declaring that the dead were dead and couldn't know who stood at the stone marking their decomposed body and casket?

Looking up with watery eyes, I saw Frau Weiss putting back the yellowing card and understood why she kept to herself: she didn't want the shared pleasure of yet another Jew discovering the details of a relative's birth any more than the sorrow at finding a burial card—or worse, not finding one, and knowing that the end had been far more grim than my grandfather's. She didn't want my tears, or anger, or even my gratitude. In this dark labyrinth of Austro-Jewish history, she had likely seen every cruel twist of recorded tragedy. If I hadn't been alone in Vienna, I would have respected her need to protect herself and gone on my way.

"I'll visit the grave tomorrow," I said shakily, and watched her shoulders shrug as she disappeared into her inner office.

Feeling too upset to leave the synagogue compound, I wandered around the empty first floor halls, eventually coming upon a heavy wooden door that led to a beautiful round mahogany-paneled temple, whose red velvet *bimah* stood under a domed ceiling of sky blue and cream. I sat crying quietly, wondering whether my supposedly easygoing grandfather could have been driven to take his own life. According to my father, Eduard had always believed his long military career would afford him protection from the Nazis. Had their disinterest in a Jewish officer weakened his spirit and his stamina? Though my father wouldn't have blamed Eduard for taking his life, knowing his desperate end might have kept my father from coming back to Vienna.

Suddenly, I heard a tinkling noise high above me: two women in
large aprons were chatting in a Slavic tongue as they wiped the crystal lamps hanging from the dome. I watched them awhile, feeling
oddly cozy in the shared dislocation that had brought each of us to
the Stadttempel.

I WAS PASSING Werdertorgasse every few days as the Ring-Kai-
Ring streetcar made its way along Franz Josefs Kai at the edge of the
Danube Canal. Looking up the narrow street, I could almost
glimpse the pale yellow building with its long ornate windows. Although something made me afraid to walk up the street and stand
at Number 9, I could tell myself that I was too busy to get off the
streetcar; besides, I had already been there with my husband Bob.

It was 1989, and we had been together over a decade when we
went to Vienna together to try to find my father's house on Werdertorgasse. In the two decades since my week with the Syrian engineering student, I had managed to learn the name of the street. Yet
I had been upset off and on since we landed at Schwechacht Airport. The imperial opulence of the great stone buildings, and the
lively chatter in Austrian German below the window of our modest
pension off Mariahilferstrasse, made me jittery, as if I were holding
back sobs, and I wondered how I would sleep the night.

In the late afternoon, I sat shivering in my sweater in an outdoor
café on the Graben, while Bob sipped his coffee and studied a map.
When he suggested a walk, I limply took his arm, as if I were an invalid. We were in a residential area, when an elderly woman in a
shapeless dark dress tripped on the curb and, despite her cane, fell
heavily. As Bob and I gathered her up and set her on her swollen an-
kles, I asked where she was going and whether she wanted us to accompany her home.

"*Ja, nach der Werdertorgasse,*" she said. Looking down at her black
laced shoes, so like my grandmother's, she tested her foot for pain.

"We'll take you. We're going there ourselves."

Unaware that she had become our guide, the old woman kept up a stream of irritable complaints about the indifference of Viennese that had left her rescue to strangers. As we approached the Vienna Stock Exchange, she pointed her cane.

Werdertorgasse. Elegant plastered apartment buildings in shades of cream lined the narrow treeless street, their large windows shining in the late afternoon sun. Number 9 was a five-story building. A dry goods store filled the ground-floor commercial space where my grandfather had sold similar merchandise during the first three decades of the twentieth century. A sign next to the carved front door showed that the Socialist Party headquarters was still in the building. Somewhere on the upper floors, in the house of his parents, my father had grown from boyhood to youth and full adulthood, an only child discovering his likes and dislikes, his talents and frailties.

I had pulled out my camera and was ready to photograph the building. But without moving farther up or down the street, and so getting Number 9 at an extreme angle, I couldn't stand far enough away to see the whole building in my lens. I heard Bob saying, "Let me try." Ready to be elsewhere, I handed him the camera and walked away.

Those photos Bob had taken in 1989 were in New York, but I thought of them each time the Ring-Kai-Ring streetcar passed Werdertorgasse. Though my anxiety was a warning that I still had business with the street, I told myself I needn't return for a second pilgrimage when I had so much research to accomplish. Not only were new tasks emerging daily as I uncovered additional possibilities to investigate, but two addresses had been added to my father's history: Grünentorgasse, Paul's birthplace, and Kolschitzkygasse, my grandparents' final lodging in Wien. I could tell myself that seeing Werdertorgasse again wasn't that important.

One afternoon during the second week of October, I was rounding the charming passageway of the Ferstl Palace, when in the window of an antique shop I saw a delicate white china cup and saucer with tiny pink flowers. Of such thin porcelain that the flowers left their shadow on the inside of the rim, the cup and saucer set my heart pounding. Among the few keepsakes Grandmother Antonie had carried out of Vienna was exactly such a tea set. Stored amidst our bright practical Fiestaware, the Viennese cups and saucers had seemed as fragile and out of place as my grandmother. Though Mother would occasionally ask me to bring them down from their high shelf when our refugee friends came for chamber music, she had regarded the tea set as an irritating inconvenience. *"Vorsichtig!"* Careful! Grandmother Antonie would watch me fearfully, as I stood on the stepstool. She didn't know that I treasured the cups as much as she did.

Standing in front of the antique shop, I wondered sadly about the apartment in which the fine porcelain had been a fitting aesthetic choice. Had there been a dark heavy glass front cabinet through which the cups could be viewed? My mother's irritations with her mother-in-law had extended beyond the china to the fox stole, embroidered linens, and Oriental carpets she had carried from Vienna in a heavy trunk—to Mother, they were all fussy, tawdry, or ornate, and out of place in the modern world. For a moment, it seemed that purchasing the cup and saucer from the antique dealer would repair the loneliness of my grandmother's terrible widowhood, and all the misunderstandings she had endured from my parents during her last years in Topeka.

Still, I resisted visiting the Werdertorgasse apartment that had housed my grandmother's flowered tea set. Even standing below the long windows seemed too close. My father wouldn't appear there to consult the weather, nor my grandmother to look down at the customers entering her husband's linen shop while she sipped her tea. Walking again along the narrow street below that pale yellow building would only reveal their terrible absence. All my mental time-traveling would suddenly come to a halt in the obvious misfortune that no Bergmann had been on the street either in sunshine or rain for fifty-five years.

8

Das Rassenbabylon

IN 1995, GRÜNENTORGASSE IN the Ninth District was a graceful residential street whose freshly painted pale yellow buildings had ornamental white cornices on the long windows. Pretty ground-floor shops stood behind a row of trees, and on the day I visited they fluttered with the last of the season's dry copper leaves. Across the street, an Italianate Catholic church, like a sugary treat in cream and beige, sat sideways in a pretty tree-filled square.

The day was too raw to stand outside Number 19, where ninety years earlier a midwife had helped my grandmother bring a baby boy into the world. After a few minutes, I found a small *Konditorei* (pastry shop) at the corner, where I sat at the window and alternated sips of bitter coffee with a sweet punch cake. Stripping the street of its gentrification, I imagined the crowded gray buildings that must have greeted Jews like the Bergmanns and Rotholzes who arrived from the Habsburg's eastern provinces toward the end of the nineteenth century. Permission to move throughout the Empire had been granted to Jews in 1849, when Eduard's and Antonie's fathers were boys. Many Jews in Bohemia and Moravia had left their villages for Prague, where my grandfather Eduard would still be banking and selling merchandise when the Nazis conducted their inventory in 1940. But Vienna's Second District of Leopoldstadt, the traditional Jewish ghetto, had soon become crowded with new arrivals, and Bohemian and Moravian Jews, including Freud's family, were moving into the Ninth District by the late nineteenth century. There is a famous story about Emperor Franz Josef from that period. Viennese were complaining that the city could absorb no more Jews. Though the aging Emperor was an antisemite when it suited his interests, the response of His Imperial Highness—"If Vienna has run out of room for Jews, they are invited to stay with me at Schönbrunn Castle."—secured the loyalty of his Jewish citizens long after his death. Even the Rotholzes apparently had their own story of the Emperor's magnanimity, as I had learned from a relative in Australia, Garry Walter. Several of Antonie's brothers were already serving in the Habsburg military when another was called up. In response, Antonie's mother, my great-grandmother, is said to have asked for an audience with the Emperor, which she was granted. When she told His Excellency that she needed this son for support, she received a dispensation.

Like Antonie's brothers, Eduard Bergmann served in the Habsburg military. Documents in the State Archives showed that he had joined a cavalry unit near Drevikov in 1893, when he was twenty. Having graduated from *Hochschule* or business school, he spoke and wrote both German and *Böhmisch* or Czech. (Since Drevikov was a predominantly Jewish village, he likely also knew Hebrew or Yiddish, but he didn't mention these languages in his induction form.) Donning the beautiful Habsburg uniform of red britches tucked into high black boots, a belted blue jacket, and a high red hat, he served for two years in the Drevikov regiment, after which his record shows him being called up nearly every year as a member of the reserves, often at a higher rank. He was in Pardobitz, east of Prague, in 1897, when the cavalry was used to quell the anti-Jewish violence sweeping Bohemia.

I don't know how Eduard came to court Antonie Rotholz, who lived in a crowded apartment a few streets away from the warm *Konditorei* where I was sitting. But he was still quartered in Pardobitz when he married her in 1903 in Magyarfalu's grand synagogue. Perhaps the couple began their marriage squeezed in with Antonie's widowed mother and the Rotholz brothers who were still at home. By the time Antonie was pregnant two years later, Eduard had joined a Mr. Reich to open his first Viennese business, a dry goods shop in Leopoldstadt, and the Bergmanns were living in the Grünentorgasse apartment.

Looking out the *Konditorei* window, I pictured Anna, the Czech wet nurse of whom my father spoke so warmly, wheeling baby Paul along the pretty street in her pram. She was hired after several unsuccessful wet nurses, including one whom Eduard was said to have routed after finding a bottle of beer under her bed. Anna then stayed on with the Bergmanns, raising Paul; and it was Anna whom my father—making her name sound like "Uhn-na"—said he had adored, rather than his mother. With half-closed eyes, I could see Anna, broad-backed in her starched white apron, as she bent over to speak soothingly to little Paul in her native tongue. Having stepped into the Catholic church across the street to light a candle for her own baby, who had been left with a village family, she would come into the *Konditorei* where I was sitting, the bell tinkling as she maneuvered her pram to select a chocolate kugel and pay for the sweet.

"*Ein süsser Bube!* With his light curls, you can't tell him from a Christian child—until you open his diaper," I could hear the shopkeeper laughing, without malice.

Except for a dark spot at the bottom of my cup, my coffee was long gone, but strong Viennese coffee forecloses a repeat. Gazing across the street at the Catholic church, I imagined Paul a few years later, kicking a ball as he waits for Anna in front of a church in the First District. Proud to be genial and open-minded, Eduard draws the line at his son going to church. Still, the nursemaid often takes Paul's hand and leads him into the dusky sanctuary to stand beside her while she prays. Then, surrounded by thick incense and cool stone, little Paul feels at once naughty and a deep comfort from this sturdy girlish woman, whose soft hand cups his as her lips move in her Czech pleas, which, she assures him, always include him!

OVER THE DIFFICULT months of 1940, my grandfather mailed a handful of old photographs as postcards to Hawaii, addressed to the new daughter-in-law he had never met. Signing the postcards simply "Papa," Eduard must have hoped to save the photos, whatever his own fate, while showing the young Berliner his son had married the proper Viennese childhood he had given Paul during the last years of Emperor Franz Josef. Though I never saw the photos while I was growing up, I had found them in an old brown envelope in my mother's buffet some months before coming to Vienna.

The earliest photo, a leafy outdoor shot, gives a window onto the extended family of Bergmanns and Rotholzes in which Paul was cared for. Antonie is mysteriously absent from the picture. Instead, sitting erect alongside Paul's aunts in their Victorian clothes, a sturdy light-haired girl in a long dark dress and large white apron holds the lace-swaddled infant. The girl's hair is pulled severely from her broad impassive face, as if to assure her employers that the fall from grace that enables her to feed the baby breast milk is behind her. Yet a softness of expression suggests outbursts of passion for her tiny ward. On the back, Eduard has written in German in his clear elegant script, "Dear Irma! A picture from June 1906, and we are curious whether you can tell who the little *Bube* is, in the arms of Anna."

The next several annual photos, carefully staged indoor shots, were taken at Palast, a photographic studio in Leopoldstadt. In a tinted mother-and-son portrait dated 1907, Antonie, in a pale blue lace blouse and long dark skirt, looks soft and lovely on an elegantly carved wooden armchair. Still hairless, Paul wears a white flowered dress, an amber necklace, and brown shoes as he sits propped next to her on a table draped in burgundy velvet. This is the only time Antonie appears alone with her son, but her relaxed warm glow suggests a pleasure and pride in her new motherhood.

Two-year-old Paul, in a sepia shot, has become a light-haired child standing alone in a long dark velvet dress with a lace collar.

Rattan garden furniture and a screen of fuzzily painted trees delineate a garden scene. A small wooden horse may be meant to remind Paul of his father's praiseworthy career as a cavalry officer. Has Eduard taught little Paul to say *Pferd*? And is the boy learning the Czech word for horse? In a memory too vague to trust, I hear my father making me laugh with a scramble of Czech sounds. Perhaps he was reciting a nursery rhyme he had learned as a child.

In the next two photographs Eduard sent my mother, young Paul is turned out in Tyrolean *Lederhosen*, a boiled wool jacket, and a mountaineering cap topped by a feather. But the sepia shot of the

Antonie, Eduard and Paul, age three

three-year-old is a family portrait, with Palast's ornately carved chair filled by Eduard in tails and a handlebar moustache. His dark eyes look bemusedly at the camera as he holds the tiny hand of the son who stands at his knees. Despite Paul's jaunty outfit, the little boy appears uncertain, as if he might turn fearfully into his father's arms. Behind Eduard, Antonie stands in a dark velvet dress with a high white lace collar, her hair swept up in elaborate wings. She looks intelligent and strong-minded, yet her ringed fingers clutch Eduard's dark sleeve, and an unpleasant thought seems to cross her mind—irritation with a bad joke her husband has just made, or with her son, who couldn't be calmed about the photographer's black cloth?

By the time Paul was five, the Bergmanns were living at 9 Werdertorgasse, and "Bergmann and Reich" had been relocated from Leopoldstadt to the ground floor of their building. The photo taken that year shows Paul in a velvet-collared coat, spats and a wide-brimmed hat that emphasizes his large ears. Although the little boy holds his walking cane with proper style, an amused turn of his mouth suggests the beginning of a double mind, both pleased and ironic to be the family's miniature dandy.

The Bergmanns had moved quickly to become Viennese residents in the prestigious First District, and in 1911 Eduard secured a Viennese *Heimatschein*, a certificate making his small family legal citizens of Austro-Hungary's capital city. Despite these signs of ambitious assimilation, a second brightly tinted studio photograph of Paul at five suggests the Bergmanns' continuing attachment to their Czech roots. An impish little boy with a satisfied smirk, arms at his hips, is wearing an elaborately embroidered Moravian village vest over a white embroidered shirt and loose white pants. On the back, where the message to my mother is dated March 1, 1940, soon after Eduard had paid the exit tax required to get out of Nazi Austria, he has sent only these words from the group house for Jews: "Dear Irma, on my birthday, I would like to give you the pleasure of imagining what this boy, in Luhatschovitz in 1911, will accomplish."

Eduard's last note to my mother, written in his careful hand shortly before he died. On the other side, Paul's costume suggests his parents' Czech origins.

9

A Military Father

THE TRACKS OF VIENNA'S U-3 line are above ground at its terminus on the southern outskirts of the city. Getting off the train one gray morning, I faced a huge McDonalds' billboard featuring a man in a Tyrolean hat ravishing his hamburger. But the bleak neighborhood of unpainted working-class apartments and industrial buildings crossed by an overhead highway might have been the unkempt sprawl surrounding any European city. Only after a moment did I see the low postwar building of ugly yellow and white tiles, in front of which a simple sign announced the State Archives of the Austrian Republic.

The photos Eduard had sent my mother showed a pampered only son on whom romantic expectations had been cast in the elegant innocence of Vienna during the last years of the Habsburg Empire. That the annual studio photos stopped abruptly with the beginning of the Great War, when my father was eight, indicated a fissure that must have shifted the ground beneath the Bergmanns once Eduard was called to war.

I deposited my jacket in one of the metal lockers provided to visitors and filled out a requisition slip at a checkout desk. I was still setting out my pencils, notebook, and German-English dictionary

on one of the long tables in a brown carpeted reading room when
several folders were miraculously set before me.

A thick purple inch-long "J" stamped on the front page of my
grandfather's military record momentarily confused my sense of
history. Then I realized that, nearly half a century after Eduard had
filled out his induction form in Drevikov and long after he had come
home from the Great War, a Nazi official had pored over the Habsburg military records in search of Jewish officers. Catching "*Mosaisch*"
on Eduard's form, he had added the stigmatizing "J" for *Jude*.

Filled out before typewriters, Eduard's annual evaluations had
been elegantly penned by Eduard's commanding officers. They
called my grandfather "*anständig*," "*gehorsam*," "*verlässich*," upright,
obedient, and reliable, and often the commanders added "*sehr*" to
emphasize their praise. "Fair," "good-natured," "loyal," "peaceful,"
and "flexible" were also regular refrains—yet how much more serious and lofty these characterizations sounded in German! Unlike
his principled son, Eduard seems to have taken life as it came, with
the easy going compliance of a successful soldier. Though he had
graduated to the cavalry reserve by the time he opened his shop in
the First District, Eduard continued to report for annual duty. "A
good model for those below him," said his superiors, as he rose in
rank, becoming one of Austro-Hungary's growing number of Jewish noncommissioned officers.

EDUARD WAS FORTY-ONE when on September 16, 1914, he was
called up to serve in the Imperial Cavalry Guard in Vienna. It was
just a month after Austro-Hungary declared war on Serbia, provoking the opposing European alliances built over decades of relative peace. Six months later, he was promoted to *Wachtmeister*
(senior sergeant), the highest noncommissioned rank and the fur-
thest a Jew could advance in the Habsburg military.

Eduard served in the Imperial Cavalry Guard as Germany, Austro-Hungary's ally, attacked France from the north, and Italy be-

trayed the Habsburgs by siding with England and France. By 1916, with cavalries rendered obsolete by tanks, bombs, trench warfare, and the first fighter planes, Eduard was assigned to Austro-Hungary's second largest prisoner of war camp in Wieselburg in central Austria. Built for 51,000 Russian and Italian prisoners, Eduard's business skills would have been critical to keeping inventory and accounts in the grocery stores, bakeries, kitchens, carpentry shops, laundry, showers, and disinfecting depot. There was also a post and telegraph office, a fire station, and several prison barracks. A hospital complex with quarantine barracks became critical as the war dragged into its third year, and with growing malnutrition prisoners succumbed to cholera, dysentery, malaria, typhus, typhoid fever, and tuberculosis. To meet the needs of Russian prisoners arriving with limbs blown off by grenades, a shop was even devoted to constructing artificial arms, legs, and feet. Literacy classes, as well as rehearsals for an orchestra, choir and theatre were all arranged to help the prisoners of war pass their free time, and the opportunity to do crafts was supposed to give prisoners products to sell or trade.

Signed by forty-one countries in 1907, the Hague Conventions stipulated rules governing the treatment of prisoners of war, from the handling of their personal effects to their food and housing (accommodations for POWs were to be appropriate to their rank). Spiritual and medical care, prisoners' rights regarding work assignments, and just compensation were also part of the regulations developed at the Hague. Although work was not to be "excessive" and prisoners were to be paid a just rate, they could be authorized to work either inside or outside the camp, in private farms and industries suffering wartime labor shortages.

Even before Eduard entered Wieselburg, however, the POW population had grown to 200,000, four times the camp's capacity. To reduce crowding, prisoners were forcibly transported to distant factories. Escapes before or during transport, along with the severe punishment of escapees, contributed to growing infractions of the Hague rules.

A sepia photograph in my packet shows Eduard in a military
tunic and high leather boots, holding his officer's sword as he sits at
the head of a mess hall table. "*Sedarfest Kriegsgefangenenlager* (Passover
Seder Prisoner-of-War camp), Wieselburg, 1916," he has written on
the white rim in his careful hand. Behind him, over thirty uni-
formed Jews of different ranks have gathered at two long wooden
tables; the officers' table is set with a white cloth, and the table for
enlisted men is set on bare wood. Though Eduard has recently been
called "good natured," "flexible," and a "good model to those below
him" by his evaluating superiors, his mustachioed face conveys only
stamina, wariness, tenacity, and grief.

In 1917, Moravian and Bohemian farmers refused to continue
supplying the Habsburgs with the grain and produce necessary to
the war effort. As hunger spread across Austria, some days no food
was available to feed prisoners in Wieselburg, and there were new
escapes, complaints from local farmers of stolen potatoes and
turnips, as well as a growing death rate inside the camp.

At midnight on Christmas Eve, December 1917, a fire broke out
in Wieselburg's administrative barracks. While the camp had an

Wachmeister Eduard Bergmann with saber (front, center). While his table is set with
a white cloth, the soldiers on the right celebrate their seder on the bare, wooden table.

active fire brigade and the alarms had always rung for previous fires, the alarm did not go off that night. When the blaze was finally extinguished, many of the camp's documents had been destroyed. Among these were records of prisoners' earnings from work assignments, as well as the deposit and cash slips for prisoners' accounts. Of some 35,000 POW deposit slips, only 2,000 could be reconstructed.

The story of Wieselburg had come to me from a meticulously researched account, *Gefangen unter Habsburgs Krone* (Prisoners under the Habsburg Crown), by an Austrian amateur historian, Franz Wiesenhofer.[3] Though the book gave rich detail to the growing desperation in the prisoner-of-war camp, Eduard's was not among the few names of officers mentioned; and hours spent with a magnifying glass, poring over the book's grainy photos of men in prison rags and Austro-Hungarian uniforms left me unable to identify my grandfather. There was no way to know whether and where Eduard had made his moral compromises and where he had stood fast— whether, for instance, he had tried to save the prisoners' accounts, or had been among those who profited from the conflagration.

I HAD ONE other photograph from the war years. It was a postcard eleven-year-old Paul had sent to *Wachtmeister* Bergmann at the POW camp around the time of the fire. The photo showed Paul in a woolen cap and ski sweater, sitting astride a sled behind his pretty older cousin, Trude Rotholz, Max's daughter. (Trude as a newlywed would immigrate to Australia, where her younger sister, Lotte, had resettled and was sending lifelines to Bergmanns and Rotholzes.) The photo was actually a studio shot with a painted backdrop of snow-covered mountains, pine trees, and a distant church steeple ; on a rock a little sign read, "Greetings from Mariazell in the year of the war, 1917."

On the back of the postcard the cousins had dictated a jovial and affectionate message:

Paul and his favorite cousin, Trude Rotholtz. My mother
added the annotation that Trude immigrated to Australia.

"Dear Papa and Uncle,

Lenke has offered to be our pen, because we are so terribly over-
worked with sledding that we don't have one minute for writing! Here
it's even more beautiful than in Semmering. It's not so exaggeratedly
comfortable as there, but it's much more cozy. And the dear God likes
us so much that the weather is heavenly!"

Though the postcard suggested an easy fondness between Eduard
and his son and niece, it raised new questions. Why, for instance,

had the cousins traveled much farther than nearby Semmering for a less "exaggeratedly comfortable" resort? Did Antonie or one of her brothers know a farmer who was able to nourish the children with fresh milk and good bread? If Antonie was in Vienna minding the store, who was Lenke? Another relative or a maid? (Garry Walter didn't know.) And what were eleven-year-old Paul's thoughts about his father's post in Wieselburg amidst hundreds of thousands of enemy prisoners?

GEFANGEN UNTER HABSBURGS KRONE contained a series of photos of the intricate woodwork carved by the Russian POWs. I had studied them now and then, but back in New York one day, while browsing through the book, I suddenly remembered a carved box with a trompe l'oeil country scene that in Topeka had stored our childhood crayons. It seemed so similar in style—could it possibly have been carved at Wieselburg? Anxious to be clear about its details, I telephoned my sister Miriam in California. As the youngest, she had been the last to use the crayon box. Impressed by the box's possible history, she agreed to search for it, and a week later she returned my call: the wooden box was at her side—she was looking at it as we spoke!

"There's writing on the sides," Miriam told me. "It must be Russian."

"So it *was* carved by a prisoner!"

Hoping that my local shoemaker, Alex, a recent immigrant from the Ukraine, could translate the words, I asked Miriam to send me the box.

"Someone has also carved inside the lid: 'PAUL BERCMANN, 1914-1917,' Miriam said.

The mistaken C for a G suggested that the Russian had copied a name he had been given in a foreign alphabet. But if Eduard had asked that the inscription be dated, the carver appeared to have recorded the length of the war, or even of his imprisonment.

"I'll let you know what I find out as soon as I get the box," I told Miriam.

A few days later, carrying the precious wooden box, I walked down Seventh Avenue to Alex's shoe repair shop. I have brought old shoes, belts, and suitcases into Alex's shop, and he has faced each of my challenges with cheerful equanimity. Now I set the box on the glass case where he sells shoelaces, shoe polish, and orthopedic inserts, and Alex and I studied the large block Russian letters.

"This is old Russian," Alex said, leaning over.

"Then you can't translate it?"

"I'm not sure."

He began to doodle. Pointing out the letters that were no longer in use, he drew lines to separate out possible words. Then, slowly, as if cornering meaning, he read,

"Wieselburg, from a Russian in captivity."

"I told you! My grandfather got it from a Russian prisoner. I mean, he probably bartered the box for food," I said, suddenly humbled by what might have been a desperate swap for a few potatoes amidst the starvation of 1917. Perhaps the Russian had been a man like the great-grandfather of Alex, or Yuri my Viennese housemate, a village Jew with whom Eduard had quietly found commonality.

Alex shook his head. "He might have been given food. But the carver intended the box as a gift." There was unusual warmth in his certainty. "You don't write 'from a Russian in captivity' unless the box is a gift. Besides," he said, "it has your father's name on the inside. Your grandfather must have talked about his son and asked to have the box inscribed."

THE LAST PHOTO Eduard sent my mother was taken on the bridge of the ship *Hamburg* in July 1920. Antonie and another woman stand in white summer dresses at the sides of the photograph, where rope ladders lead at a slant to the mast. Antonie seems subdued and worn, and a weary line at the edge of her mouth prefigures the grandmother I would know. Eduard looks beefy and stiff in a dark civilian suit and high collar; and the scowl on his face shows that his well-recorded good nature could give way to stubborn displeasure.

But it is fourteen-year-old Paul, standing in a sailor suit at the ship's wheel, who particularly interests me. His bright eagerness is edged with anxiety, as if he is not sure he is up to the responsibilities of steering.

The Bergmanns were on their way to Helgoland, an island off the northern coast of Germany, as Eduard wrote on the back of the last picture he sent my mother in late 1940. He said the photo recalled *"eine schoener Zeit."* Remembered while sitting in the crowded Kolschitzky-gasse apartment, the Helgoland trip must have seemed "a nicer time." Helgoland had been a major German fortification, but the Treaty of Versailles had forced Germany to demilitarize, and the island was suddenly open to visitors. Perhaps, too, from his confinement in the group home, the anti-Semitism that had surged across Austria in response to the Habsburg's defeat twenty years earlier seemed fairly harmless. Many blamed both the "Jewish profiteers" who made war materiel, and the "Jewish socialists" who agreed to the truncated boundaries of the new Austria. As civilians taunted returning soldiers, and pogroms threatened Leopoldstadt, Jewish soldiers formed a volunteer corps to protect the Second District. In 1920, Eduard's and Antonie's native Bohemian and Slovakian villages were in the new independent country of Czechoslovakia. With Austrian resorts rejecting Jewish vacationers,[4] the Bergmanns might have conceived of the trip north into Germany as an interesting solution to a holiday.

Some of this sad history I read into Antonie's weariness and Eduard's glower, for how could they not suffer from Austria's isolation and defeat at the end of four long years of war. Yet, perhaps as Eduard prepared to send the photo from Kolschitzkygasse to his daughter-in-law, what he saw was not the strain of the war and its aftermath, but only the precocious and puzzling son he still adored.

1 0

The Renunciation

DOING ARCHIVAL RESEARCH demands both discipline and a kind of looseness of the intellect. Since libraries contain unanticipated information, one moves back and forth in time, proceeding by instinct, a little like free-associating, as one follows leads that turn into tangents or create chronological loops and yield unanticipated discoveries. Throughout my October in Vienna, I kept returning to Frau Heidi Weiss at the Israëlitische Kultusgemeinde. In the archives of the Austrian Resistance Movement, I had discovered Bergmanns and Rotholzes deported to Theresienstadt, the "model" concentration camp outside Prague—and I walked back to the narrow cobblestone street to see if any of these individuals might be relatives my father had never mentioned. One was my father's uncle, my grandmother's older brother Jakob, an upholsterer—another reason for her pinched solitude during her last years in Topeka, and perhaps for my father's abiding rage at his native city. (Antonie's four other brothers died before the *Anschluss*.)

The recently computerized Jewish cemetery plots in the Zentralfriedhof also suggested potential family members on whom I wanted to check. Was the Sophie Bergmann buried in the cemetery my father's grandmother? No, as it turned out. Having found Vienna's annual address books from the early decades of the twentieth century in the National Library, I was tracing Eduard's business: the linen shop he opened with Mr. Reich in Leopoldstadt in 1905; its move to Werdertorgasse several years later; Mr. Reich's eventual departure from the shop, which Eduard then owned alone until 1931, when he bought a sock and tie factory in the suburb of Penzing, a ten-minute walk from Schönbrunn Castle, where Emperor Franz Josef had ceremoniously invited Vienna's unwanted Jews. Sorrowfully, in 1940 the Emperor had been dead for over two decades, and his benevolent ghosts had been unable to protect my grandfather's factory.

Yet my returns to the Kultusgemeinde were prompted as much by inner disarray as by the logic of my progressing research: despite my effort to proceed carefully in a balanced frame of mind, I was getting snagged by those subterranean fears my daytime diligence generally blanketed. One rainy morning, I asked Frau Weiss to bring down the birth book so that I could photograph the handwritten page about Paul; but a week later, standing in a photo shop to have the film developed, I discovered that my camera had been empty.

Though I was becoming familiar with the security precautions of the synagogue complex, each time I buzzed the front doorbell the Israeli guards subjected me to the same brusque impersonal search; and though Frau Weiss nodded in vague recognition when I entered, she gave me no sense that she was becoming interested in my work. With less warmth than a waitress in a busy luncheonette (her two rooms were nearly always empty), she filled each order and quickly disappeared until I called to her with a new request.

On my fourth visit, having yet again taken down the heavy leather-bound 1906 birth book, Frau Weiss paused to study Paul Bergmann's record with detached curiosity. After a moment, she tapped the right side of the large page.

"He renounced Judaism in 1924," she said curtly, her finger with its chipped rose polish drumming the page. "Look here, it says, 'September 1924, *aus dem Judentum ausgetreten.*'"

Renounced Judaism? The handwritten notation under the column head denoting the circumcision day and child's Hebrew name swam before my eyes. Like a criminal awaiting my own verdict, I tried to focus on the terrible disclosure. Whatever disturbing revelations I might have been afraid of uncovering about my father's Viennese past, I had never suspected this.

I had been raised as a Jew. Stripped of its enriching liturgy and observances, being a Jew had seemed a grim heritage, marked only by centuries of persecution, culminating in our near extinction. If I had played at passing in the country club as a teenager, I never considered not being Jewish. Converting to another faith, or denying that I was a Jew, was unthinkable—which was why my obfuscation in the police precinct still overwhelmed me with shame.

Through my upset, I heard Frau Weiss explaining in her tired matter-of-fact voice that nearly a third of the records of Viennese born in the first decades of the century were marked, "withdrawal from Judaism." A scholar who was making a study of these renunciations was finding so many that it would be long before she was through. Some Jews, considering themselves modern and scientific, assumed that every life and death question would soon have an empirical answer. Some were socialists building a secular paradise here on earth. And, of course, simple ambition drove many. Though no one forgot that you were born a Jew, you had to be a Catholic to get anywhere—lawyers converted to become judges, doctors for hospital appointments. Gustav Mahler had converted to Catholicism to be able to conduct the Vienna Philharmonic Orchestra. Even Otto Bauer, the Socialist leader between the wars, had become a Protestant to enhance his political authority.

"My father might have wanted a career as a pianist or university professor," I said, following her line of thought. My face was hot with shame as I scrambled to calculate how old he had been in 1924.

"Don't think anything of it," Frau Weiss replied. "He probably had to do it."

I tried to imagine Paul leaving Judaism to advance his ambitions. Did the motive fit? He had been only eighteen! Wouldn't a righteous principle, rather than a careful career strategy, have been more characteristic of my father, particularly as a young man? Thirty years later, when I was in my late teens, he showed only disdain for using influence and connections, relying on patronage, or shifting one's artistic or intellectual project to satisfy a public. When he talked about Gustav Mahler, it was with a critical edge—for my father saw a connection between his great-uncle prettifying his identity for his orchestral ambitions and his overwrought self-aggrandizing symphonies. When I applied to Vassar, my father was upset that, Carol Ross, after whom I had been named, insisted on writing to the college in my behalf. He wanted my opportunities to arise out of merit, or not at all.

Could the memory of deserting one's heritage feel so squalid that it left one unbending about daily compromise? Or had a righteous rigidity, unwilling to go along with propriety and custom, been Paul's boyhood way of separating from the conformity of his hard-driving, anxious mother and his compliant military father?

Frau Weiss was tapping her short finger a little further along the line.

"It says he came back. *Rücktritt, 2 Februar 1934*."

The new information of his return ten years later should have been reassuring.

"Why?" I asked shakily.

"A lot of people did that once they saw that the Nazis considered anyone without four Aryan grandparents a Jew. The books show two waves of returns: the first in 1934, after Hitler assumed power in Germany and Austria's brief civil war replaced the social democratic government with Christian fascism, and the second after the *Anschluss* in 1938, when Austria became a province of the Third Reich."

I could have focused on my father's early return to the fold; instead, it was his rejection of Judaism that held me in its grip, and left me feeling as if the ground had shifted beneath my feet. Walking around Vienna's damp and chilly streets, I tried out different narratives to explain Paul's youthful decision not to be a Jew. Might Eduard have been the instigator? A practical man, he would have experienced how a Jew had to work harder in the military, and witnessed the many obstacles to a Jew's business success. Yet it was Eduard who had celebrated Passover at Wieselburg, making his Judaism a public event. Moreover, if Eduard had suggested such insincerity to his son, wouldn't I have glimpsed a lingering resentment in my father's attitude toward his father? Perhaps Antonie had suggested that Paul convert. Antonie, with her Viennese worries and pretensions, had likely been the more easily dissatisfied parent. If so, my father's lingering shame could have fueled the irritation at his mother I saw as a child. And there was beloved Anna, who must have influenced him with her simple religious devotion.

Yet the handwritten entry in the birth book stated only that Paul was formally leaving Judaism, not moving toward another faith.

In the afternoon a cool autumn sun came out. As I walked along the Danube Canal, I remembered a description of Paul by Sonia Wachstein, an old Viennese girlfriend I had discovered in New York. They had been together for a while during their university years, and, like many other Jewish students, Sonia said they had both been socialists. "We were all socialists in those days! That was our world!" Studying to become an actress, Sonia had even performed political cabaret for the Social Democratic Party in Vienna's working class districts. Yet she remembered my father as the zealot.

"Paul, he was a madman! He and his Marxism—and his psychoanalysis! It was either one or the other," she had laughed, her voice deep from years of cigarettes. "He didn't leave you alone. He was messianic!"

Sonia made me see my father as a hot-headed young man, consumed by the still innocent dream of an egalitarian world, rational, freed from all superstition. Romantic, stubborn, rash, this Paul was as impatient with Inner City Jews like his parents, whose Judaism was limited to shutting their shops on Saturday, keeping kosher, and attending synagogue on the High Holidays, as he was with the Hasidic Jews of Leopoldstadt, who drove themselves into fervent prayer several times a day and clung to their eighteenth century rituals and clothing.

Paul had invited Sonia to the Werdertorgasse apartment to hear him play the piano, and she had been impressed by his great talent. All Jewish sons and daughters of ambitious parents took music lessons in those days, but Paul had really made something of it! Still, she remembered teasing him: How did wanting to master Beethoven's *Hammerklavier* fit in with his revolutionary program?

I could imagine Eduard, at home in the evenings, alternately teasing and irritable about the dog-eared copies of Marx and Kautsky and Rosa Luxemburg that crowded Paul's desk and spilled out of his bookshelf. Calling Paul *"mein vogelfreier Kerl,"* his outlaw kid, Eduard might have insisted that he too wanted peace and bread on everyone's table. Which was exactly what the Social Democratic Party, whose compromises so irked Paul, was carefully trying to build.

But it would have been Antonie's sentimental memories of the Emperor, which I still glimpsed in the 1940s, as well as her endless dissatisfactions and petty scheming, which made the messages of the radical left increasingly attractive to Paul. Taking advantage of the deflation, she had even acquired her own apartment building in a working-class district, which she intended to rent out for additional income. I could hear him angrily paraphrasing Marx to her: "Landlords are parasites!" How he would have longed for a world where everyone had useful and decently paid work, and neither religion nor the family held its crippling grip!

On a warm Monday afternoon, after a Sunday visit from the Rotholzes, with their endless talk of sales, reductions, and profits, Paul must have crossed the park at Rudolfsplatz and walked with determined strides to Seitenstättengasse. The scribe at the Israëlitische Kultusgemeinde, a servile, hunched, withered man, thin gray hairs peeking from his yarmulke, was exactly the kind of Jew who made Paul's flesh crawl. He waited, hands in pockets, as the man shuffled over to the cupboard where the large birth books were stored. The old Jew had opened the book when he suddenly turned his yellowing face toward Paul with aggression. "What will your father do when he understands that he no longer has a son who can say *Kaddish* for him?"

Paul glared silently. And a moment later, the old Jew had set his pen to the page. *Aus dem Judentum ausgetreten.* The book was barely back on the shelf when Paul had turned to the door. Walking quickly toward the Danube, in a mood of angry exaltation, he stretched his legs. This, finally this, marked his solitary manhood, as all the nonsense he had memorized for his bar mitzvah never could do.

11

The Force of Ideas

IN A REVERSAL OF FREUD'S HURRIED flight to London from Vienna in June 1938, I had stopped briefly in London to visit Freud's home in exile on my way to Vienna. My widowed mother remembered Paul taking her as a newlywed to visit Sigmund Freud at Maresfield Gardens in the late winter of 1939. To her, Freud seemed both imposing and frail (he would die several months later, having suffered cancer of the jaw for years). She didn't recall what they had talked about—she herself had probably been too awed to speak. But Paul had wanted Freud to meet his new wife, and to know that he was safely out of Vienna and would soon leave for Hawaii, thanks to a visa from an American who had been psychoanalyzed in Vienna.

Sigmund Freud had resisted fleeing Vienna; only after his daughter Anna's second arrest by the Gestapo had he consented to allow psychoanalysts in France and England to help resettle the family. Since Freud was internationally famous, he was made to sign a paper confirming that he had been well treated. "I am happy to give the Gestapo my best recommendation," he wrote, with dark Viennese humor that could have been my father's. His four older sisters, who remained in Vienna, would perish in concentration camps.

Maresfield Gardens is a leafy London street, and the red brick Georgian house at Number 20 is both intimate and stately. With

147

some of the comfortable rooms retaining vestiges of the Freud family's decor, and others used for educational exhibitions and archival storage, the house, which has become the Freud Museum, is sunny, airy and pretty, a cheerful place to visit.

I was met at the door by the lanky long-haired archivist, Michael Muldane, wearing jeans and a sports shirt. Chatting amiably, he showed me around. Since I had written that I hoped to learn about my father's involvement in the movement for psychoanalytic pedagogy, he soon pulled from a file drawer a folder containing the minutes of the Teaching Institute of the Vienna Psychoanalytic Society during the inter-war years, and sent me upstairs to work at leisure.

Sitting alone at a wooden trestle table in the charming yellow attic that had been Anna Freud's bedroom, I pored over the minutes of the Teaching Institute's monthly administrative meetings. Amateurishly typed, with a ribbon usually in need of replacement, the terse German offered a view onto those decisions that the half-dozen now famous psychoanalysts constituting the administrative committee—Helene Deutsch, Paul Federn, Anna Freud, Eduard Hitchmann, Hermann Nunberg, Wilhelm Reich, and Theodor Reik—had thought worthy of record.

On the 11th of November 1926, two years after Paul became *Konfessionslos*, and shortly after Vienna's Social Democratic city government honored Freud on his seventieth birthday by donating a parcel of land for the Psychoanalytic Society's headquarters, the minutes contained the following entry:

> Paul Bergmann, Pädagoge, Univ. can. für Lehramtsprüfung, mit Bernfeld bekannt, will nicht Analytiker werden, nur in seiner Schulpraxis anwenden; kann nicht zahlen.

The entry contradicted my mother's story that Paul had become an analyst to understand the growing attraction of fascism to his students—a story that had the logic of pointing to my father's interest in the psychology behind any unsavory political position. But the 1926 entry showed that Paul had entered the world of psycho-analysis before he began teaching and nearly a decade before the rise of fascism. As Paul told the committee, he was in the university, working toward his teaching examination; he wanted analytic train-ing for his future work as a teacher, not to practice psychoanalysis. He also explained that he was unable to pay for the training. Since he was living at home and relying on his hard-working parents for expenses, he must have hoped not to involve them in his contro-versial and highly personal adventure, which would likely raise old complaints and unacknowledged desires in a psychoanalysis.

Yet Paul's use of Siegfried Bernfeld as a reference gave some sup-port to politics being implicated in his reasons for deciding to enter the world of psychoanalysis. Ten years Paul's senior, Bernfeld had begun attending lectures at the Vienna Psychoanalytic Society in 1913 and had received a doctorate in psychology from the Univer-sity of Vienna two years later. But his psychological interests arose within Zionist, pacifist, and socialist commitments. With the out-break of war in 1914, Bernfeld's antiwar speeches drew large crowds of young students, including those Paul's age. Believing that adults were materialistic and hypocritical, Bernfeld used his writings, an edited journal, and direct organizing to build groups of Jewish youth that were communitarian, antimaterialist, and prepared to build a new Jewish society in Palestine.[5] In 1918, as the Russian in-vasion of the eastern lands of the Habsburg Empire brought grow-ing numbers of orphaned Jewish youth to Vienna, Bernfeld opened Kinderheim Baumgarten, a home for some two hundred youth gov-erned by libertarian and psychoanalytic principles. Although the orphanage failed after six months (the American funder pulled out and Bernfeld came down with tuberculosis), Bernfeld's Kinderheim Baumgarten[6] would influence progressive child welfare in Austria and the developing kibbutz movement in Palestine. In 1919, Bern-feld and Willi Hoffer, who would also become a psychoanalyst, opened the Jewish Institute for the Study of Adolescence to investi-gate issues of psychology and pedagogy among Jewish youth.[7]

Bernfeld was Martin Buber's secretary in 1920 when he underwent psychoanalysis and became a lay analyst and an active member of the Vienna Psychoanalytic Society. Sobered by the advent of protofascist paramilitary veterans' groups, which showed that the autonomous youth organizations he had imagined for the Left could develop with right-wing ideologies, Bernfeld settled into a more private life. He was one of the main lecturers in the Society's Teaching Institute in 1926, when he must have told Paul to use his name with the administrative committee.

Using anyone as a reference was unlikely to have been a casual matter for Paul, and I had to take Bernfeld's name seriously. But what did it reveal? If Paul had been a follower of Bernfeld during the war years, his ambivalence toward his military father had been deeper and earlier than I supposed. Becoming *Konfessionslos* at eighteen would then have meant a violent turning away from both his parents' expedient Jewish observances and Bernfeld's intense efforts to develop a new Jewish identity. And Paul's interest in psychoanalysis implied an attempt at some kind of rapprochement with Judaism, his parents, and Bernfeld.

Perhaps Paul was a university student who had already taken his stand for a secular socialist society when he met Bernfeld. Paul must have been attracted by Bernfeld's critical view of adults. Yet even visiting Bernfeld's institute or attending a Bernfeld meeting or lecture suggested a willingness to engage with a Jewish viewpoint Paul had supposedly rejected.

Though there was no way to know the depth of the relationship between the two men, it was tempting to imagine them walking the cobblestone streets of Vienna as they discuss the political and philosophical questions that absorb them. Bernfeld, who is a head taller than Paul, smokes incessantly and his gaunt good looks have begun to age, but both men have thick black hair and angular faces, and both are uncomfortably thin beneath worn woolen suits. Though Paul is circumspect, he allows Bernfeld to understand the idealistic hope (as well as distaste for his family) that caused him to leave Judaism, and his surprise at his continuing discomfort with an act that was supposed to bring release and the pride of self-determination. Bernfeld intuits the anguish from which Paul's confession has arisen and is careful with the younger man. Somehow the two come to the conclusion that Paul may find it interesting to explore his psyche and assist in developing a progressive pedagogy by entering the Psychoanalytic Society's Teaching Institute, where, Bernfeld assures him, he will be viewed as a good fit and will have no trouble being admitted.

ANNA FREUD WAS teaching in one of Vienna's day care centers for children when she visited Bernfeld at Kinderheim Baumgarten and August Aichhorn at Ober-Hollabrunn, the experimental home for juvenile delinquents he had founded and was directing for the city of Vienna. The three had begun meeting regularly in an informal study group, where they conceived of a discipline of psychoanalytic pedagogy. Austria's public education system, in the view of most progressives, prepared its students for the obedience and social passivity needed by authoritarian regimes. To build socialist democracy, a new group of teachers needed to be trained, who could offer a more open pedagogy that prepared thoughtful and responsible citizens. Influenced by psychoanalysis, Anna Freud, who was best at articulating the potential of psychoanalysis for improving education, went a step further. Psychoanalysis, she believed, could extend educators' knowledge of the complicated relationships between children and adults. It could also show that in each of the three developmental stages—childhood, latency, and adolescence—there was a "middle ground" between children's need for drive gratification and drive control; thus, psychoanalysis could critique existing pedagogical methods, showing "the injurious effect of excessive interference" on the one hand, and the harm done by "lack of restraint" on the other. Finally, psychoanalysis could "repair the injuries inflicted upon the child during the process of a conventional education."[8]

In 1924, as the Psychoanalytic Society's Training Institute offered a track for psychoanalytic pedagogues for the first time, Vienna's Social Democratic city government was attempting to ameliorate the capital's lingering post-war poverty with ambitious programs of low-cost public housing; public hospitals, parks, baths, and kindergartens; child welfare programs for the poor; as well as workers' education programs and the transformation of the Habsburg Catholic school system into a new system of secular public education.[9] "Not the idea of force, but the force of ideas," was the slogan of Austria's Social Democrats, who believed that the programs they were creating in Vienna would lead to a national electoral vote for socialism, and so avoid the violence of the Russian revolution.

The London Freud Museum contained the annual catalogues of the Psychoanalytic Society's Teaching Institute between Winter 1924 and Spring 1938, two months after the *Anschluss*, when the Hitler regime closed the Psychoanalytic Society. Catalogues from the period when my father began his training show an introduction to psychoanalytic psychology by Siegfried Bernfeld, and to dream theory by Eduard Hitchmann. Wilhelm Reich, Paul Federn, Otto Rank, and Felix Deutsch offered courses to prospective analysts, which were also open to those in the psychoanalytic pedagogic track. Prospective psychoanalytic pedagogues were required to take a course on the delinquent child by August Aichhorn, who had recently published a book on his work at Ober-Hollabrunn. *Verwarloste Jugend*[10] (*Wayward Youth*) presents case studies of Aichhorn's treatment of a handful of delinquent adolescents using insight and other psychoanalytic techniques, making it clear that punishment, the commonly used strategy, was ineffective. Another required course, on the psychoanalysis of child neurosis, was given by Hermine Hug-Helmuth, who had invented play therapy.

Psychoanalytic pedagogues were also required to obtain practical experience in using analytic insight as a tool for education and "re-education" at one of Vienna's day treatment or residential centers for children. (After 1932, when Aichhorn retired from the city system, internships were held at the Child Guidance Center of the Vienna Psychoanalytic Society, whose adolescent program he directed.)

Finally, all students training to be psychoanalytic pedagogues were required to undergo psychoanalysis, supposedly less intense than that needed for analytic work with neurotic patients.

A FEW DAYS after my visit to Maresfield Gardens, I was installed in Mrs. V.'s large cluttered room in Vienna and was visiting the museum and archives of the Vienna Psychoanalytic Society, my first research task in Vienna. Whereas the Freud Museum in London, with its wide windows overlooking a pretty, tree-filled garden, conveys Anna Freud's cheerful order, even her faith in "normalcy," the museum and archives of the Vienna Psychoanalytic Society are housed in Sigmund Freud's apartment on Berggasse, a dreary cobblestone street of gray five-story residential buildings. On that drizzly Yom Kippur day, the somberness of the second-floor apartment was accentuated by tourists quietly walking through the consulting rooms, as if the father of psychoanalysis were himself lying in state. Perhaps Freud's forced flight from his home, where he had mourned the premature death of his oldest daughter, Sophie, had come to his understanding of the darker instincts driving human behavior, and had continued to feel like an outsider, despite a growing circle of loyal colleagues, was casting added shadows on this day of Jewish repentance.

I was apprehensive about approaching the world of Viennese psychoanalysis, from which my father had shaped an argumentative and peripatetic American career. Somehow the theory as much as the practice of psychoanalysis also seemed to embody something about our relationship, his and mine—about our intimacy and blurred boundaries, and my father's vain attempts to name motives and feelings in the hope of defeating the insecurity, rage and passion that at times flowed between us.

That morning the paucity of documents in the archive catalogue bearing the name Paul Bergmann stung me with raw shame. I wanted my father to have made his way into the archival history of the Vienna Psychoanalytic Society, to validate the aura of greatness in which I had once bathed him. Yet, just as he had mistrusted my capacities, I was suspicious of his feet of clay, and the fact that there were a dozen entries for a Theresa Bergmann, and only a few for Paul, seemed to give new evidence of his marginality, even his failure. As I swung between hope for some kind of confirmation of my childish adoration and fear of humiliation in his behalf, it never occurred to me that the absence of files in his name reflected the small and haphazard collection, resurrected piecemeal after the war, and the scarcity of *any* records connected to the Teaching Institute, and particularly to the courses in psychoanalytic pedagogy and those who had studied in this track.

In fact, a shy young dark-haired woman had appeared briefly to offer me a way to continue my research: the grandson of August Aichhorn lived in the Ninth District. Thomas Aichhorn was himself a psychoanalyst and had his grandfather's papers. Moreover, he was interested in the lost history of psychoanalytic pedagogy, and would likely share his information with me. Withdrawing to her office to check the address and phone number, she handed them to me on a slip of paper.

But I was apprehensive about introducing myself in German to a stranger on the telephone, moreover to an Austrian analyst. The very prospect elicited all my old insecurities. Then one evening when Yuri was home, I succumbed to his strict mentoring and wrote Aichhorn a note filled with the Viennese courtesies that my Russian housemate had mastered in the hope of building a successful career as a violinist. As the days went by without a response, I wondered if my own forthright Americanized German might have sounded more authentic; but I was also relieved to go about my research tasks without meeting this man whose eerily close lineage to Paul seemed capable of changing my image of my father and so felt threatening to me.

———————

FOR FREUD AND the Psychoanalytic Society, the Teaching Institute was a way to expand the involvement of professionals in psychoanalysis. While the analytic track actualized Freud's belief that psychoanalysts should include those with literary and humanistic, not just medical, backgrounds, the track in psychoanalytic pedagogy was an attempt to involve teachers and social workers in implementing the social and political goals of a socialist democracy. While the offerings in both tracks were careful and orderly, the shorter sequence (along with a less extensive analysis) offered to psychoanalytic pedagogues suggested that graduates of that track would hold a secondary status within the Psychoanalytic Society. Reinforcing this lower status, the young students, public school teachers, and social workers who entered the track in psychoanalytic pedagogy were a lively and restless group. Unlike the analysts in Freud's inner circle, or those lay analysts he hoped to train, the young teachers and social workers were generally too unruly to become devotees of a single theoretical system.

Edith Buxbaum, a Viennese *Gymnasium* teacher who resettled in Seattle, becoming a child analyst, looked back on the pedagogic track in this way: "The first thing you got was that you were allowed to go to lectures. Then you were allowed to go to Society meetings, where the 'big shots' were." The tongue-in-cheek may have been provoked by envy, but it also suggested a rebellious spirit. Buxbaum continued, "Actually, whenever there was anybody who gave a lecture, you would go." Buxbaum also joined Wilhelm Reich's Socialist Society for Sexual Advice and Sexual Research. She recalled, "We went to all the lectures there were. We practically went five nights a week."[11]

I had visited Rudi Ekstein, one of my father's few remaining Viennese colleagues, shortly before coming to Vienna. Like Paul, Rudi had spent some years in Topeka at the Menninger Sanitarium. But he had moved to Los Angeles around the time we left for Seattle. In 1995, the wide windows of Rudi's house opened onto exotic tropical vegetation, but inside Rudi's radical past was obscured by the heavy hardcover volumes filling the dark high bookcases, and a dense display of old photographs and etchings of Freud, the Viennese Psychoanalytic Society in the years between the two World Wars, and old Viennese streets.

A portly old man with striking olive skin against a thick head of silver hair, Rudi greeted me in a worn cardigan, baggy slacks and slippers. As he lowered himself into the heavy leather chair in which he still saw patients, he immediately began to reminisce. A few years younger than Paul, he recalled them sitting next to each other in the psychology classes of Karl and Charlotte Bühler at the University of Vienna. The Bühlers had opened a cognitive psychology laboratory, and were presenting the newest theories of child development to Viennese *Gymnasium* teachers. He also recalled Paul from Moritz Schlick's philosophy class. Schlick, the logical positivist, had taught them the intellectual caution of asking, "What do you mean when you say . . ?" It was this careful, at times brutal, search for truth that reminded Rudi of Paul.

"Paul could stay with truthful thinking, but not with any final truth," Rudi said, shaking his large head with respect for my father. Like Paul, Rudi admired Schlick, but as the only child of a widowed father, he needed to be part of a fervent group of believers. He even joined the *Schutzbund,* the paramilitary wing of the Social Democratic Party, and his days were filled with the urgency of defending the fragile Republic. Comparing his youthful choices to Paul's led him to remember Topeka, where Paul became a critic of psychoanalysis, and he again sided with the True Believers.

"Tell me more about your studies," I broke in, wanting to constrain the wide loops of Rudi's memories.

"*Ach,* our university years! What rich learning we had, what great hope for ourselves and humanity! How this could have been, when the fascist students were waiting outside the class, taunting us, '*Juden hinaus! Juden hinaus!*' Jews get out!" Rudi chuckled. "It must have focused our minds, knowing that at the end of the hour we would have to fight our way to safety." Suddenly, Rudi broke into a rowdy song,

Braun gebrannt sind wir und verwegen!
Deswegen haben die Mädchen uns so gern!

We're tanned and courageous,
Which is why the girls love us!

Stopping short, he smiled rambunctiously, "Well, that was me—not really your father. He knew his Marx, but he wasn't in the *Schutzbund,* and his life wasn't the Party like mine was. Socialism was probably more aesthetic or ethical for him."

IN APRIL 1927, five months after Paul applied to the Psychoanalytic Society's Teaching Institute, Austria's Social Democratic Party won its largest electoral victory since the onset of the Republic in 1918. Some believed that Austria would avoid the Soviet Union's revolutionary bloodbaths by finding a peaceful democratic transition to socialism. But on July 15, two members of a rightist paramilitary organization, the Heimwehr, were acquitted of murdering the eight-year-old son of a railway worker and an unemployed member of the Schutzbund. As news of the acquittal spread through Vienna, hundreds of thousands stormed the Palace of Justice, which was soon in flames.

Each time I read about the surge of angry protesters, I saw Paul somewhere in its midst. Running along with the other demonstrators. Calling to a girlfriend who had momentarily disappeared in the panicked mass. Running again, this time terrified as police shots from the Palace of Justice cracked near his head. (But, of course, Paul might have been away from Vienna, studying in Paris, or visiting with relatives in Drevikov.) Belatedly, the Social Democratic Party sent *Schutzbundlers* like Rudi to stand between the police and the demonstrators. But they were armed with only batons, and stood by helplessly, fodder for the shots that whizzed by. At the end of that day, ninety Viennese were dead and hundreds were wounded.[12]

Rudi bitterly recalled how Otto Bauer and other socialist leaders had been too afraid of confrontation; for Rudi, the slaughter at the Palace of Justice was needless proof that an unarmed and defensive socialist militia made no sense. But Paul had a more fastidious and ambivalent nature: even had he once believed that that the Social Democratic Party would need to engage in violence as it took over the apparatuses of the state, the bloodbath would likely have over-reached his tolerance for revolutionary slaughter.

In late 1927, Paul was finally assigned to begin analysis with Dr. Ludwig Jekels, a sixty-year-old Polish Jewish neurologist, who had come to Vienna after running a sanitarium for neurotic clients in Bistrai. One of the more conservative members of Freud's early loyal circle, Jekels was translating Freud's work into Polish. He was a dignified man of great integrity, and a Communist who had writ-ten a book on Marxism and Freud, which may be why the adminis-trative committee thought him an appropriate analyst for Paul.

I imagine young Paul with his high-pitched nerves and well-trained mind, stretching out on Jekels's analytical couch. Having studied the classics of philosophy and literature, Paul has become an obsessive reader of political thinkers. Even the tracts of Zionist-socialists whirl in his twenty-one-year-old head. Though Bernfeld has assured him of Jekels's analytic skill, Paul's instinct is to mock the elderly man, whose silences seem as pompous and authoritar-ian as his political views. Can Paul trust Jeckels sufficiently to nar-rate his own deep story?

Paul speaks with caution about his father, who has been an up-standing soldier, businessman and citizen, even if he jokes too much, sometimes cuts corners, and can't always be trusted with his arithmetic. Then, suddenly, in a rush of bitter relief, his mother fills his mind. This mother who has always handled her husband's ac-counts—Oh, she doesn't miss a pfennig!—and now she adds to the family income with her own rental business. How she sucks him and his father into her bottomless anxieties! How she infects them both with her fears and ambitions!

Paul's relationship with Jekels was likely uncomfortable and his analysis must have been prematurely terminated, for a few years later the records of the Psychoanalytic Society note that Paul has been assigned to a second analyst, this time Otto Isakower,[13] a younger member of the Viennese Psychoanalytic Society who has written a book of poetry.

IN THE BACK of my mother's linen closet, I had discovered a dense German essay on the unconscious, poorly-typed on onionskin. The essay, which attempted to offer systematic and scientific evidence for the existence of an unconscious, was unlikely to have been popular on Berggasse, where loyal psychoanalysts generally did not press for the need to buttress their new discipline with either experimental psychology or logical positivism. But it confirmed Rudi Ekstein's memory of seeing Paul in the cognitive psychology of classes of the Bühlers and Moritz Schlick's lectures on logical positivism.

A small group of Viennese had actually attempted to translate Freud's *Group Psychology and the Analysis of the Ego* into logical positivist language during the inter-war years. Though another member of the group would describe the work as "totally frustrating,"[14] Paul's essay seemed likely to have been part of that project.

The gap between psychoanalysis and empiricist psychology would come to seem more bridgeable outside Vienna. In London, Anna Freud and several refugee researchers trained under the Bühlers would use psychoanalytic theory to observe children at the Hempstead nurseries. And with a Menninger colleague, Sibylle Escalona, Paul would combine psychoanalytic theory with empirical research to study infants and children in Topeka.[15]

IT WAS MY third week in Vienna, and, having had several unpleasant arguments over the house phone, I often barely nodded as Yuri rushed passed me in the suddenly perfumed hall, his violin case banging against his side. One evening I returned to find his scribbled message:

"T. Aichhorn called."

A violin concerto was blaring from the CD player on the other side of his closed door. Trembling with sudden fury at the skimpy message, I knocked, then knocked a little louder. The music was turned down, and Yuri's face appeared in a crack in the door.

"You didn't take down Aichhorn's phone number," I snapped. "How am I supposed to call him back?"

Yuri looked wounded as he tried to close the door on me. "He'll probably call again . . ."

"Yuri, I've taken down dozens of numbers for you!" This was so true it didn't need elaboration; nevertheless, I continued, "Girlfriends, agents, music teachers, even calls from Moscow. I should have told every damn one of them to call again!"

My rage was demeaning and useless. After I cooled down, I realized that I could look up Aichhorn in the Viennese telephone book, and several days later I remembered the slip of paper I'd received at the Freud Museum. But I waited to see if Aichhorn would call again.

Sons of the Revolution

L ONG AFTER HIS DEATH, MY father remained the severe
judge of my achievements. The internal equation I maintained was simple and constant, if not in my best interests:
by obscuring my successes, I kept him elevated in my private pantheon, and my rejections and failures could always be used to echo
his measure of the distance between what I could accomplish and
anything of worth. Yet in Vienna I was glimpsing a fragile, change-
able young man, driven by wounds, principle, and ambition—not
exactly the Zeus I had known and kept alive. My Vienna was surely
different than his had been—more paint on the stately buildings,
more goods in the little shops, more money everywhere. Still, I
could glimpse how the extremity of his aspirations had developed
amidst unparalleled civil violence and vast social dreams. Even in
Vienna, he had been both eager to make his great social contribution, and willing to declare an effort unworthy or not exactly what
was needed, and begin again.

One morning, about to change underground trains at the Schottentor station at the University of Vienna, I impulsively climbed out
of the U-Bahn station to look for his doctoral dissertation in the
university archives. No one guarded the university's grand main
gate, and I was inside the complex of Renaissance-style buildings

before I realized I didn't know the rules for visitors. Cautiously, I began to explore the wide marble hallways that led to heavy wooden doors, graceful stairways, porticoes, and serenely landscaped inner courts. I had seen signs for the library, but I almost passed its small inconspicuous door on the second floor. Inside, like Alice in Wonderland, I wandered from one substantial book-lined room to another in a vast inner world of which the hallway had given me no inkling. Finally, approaching a stocky light-haired librarian bent over a book, I said that I was looking for a doctoral dissertation, probably completed sometime in the 1930s.

"Name?" the young man jumped to his feet.

We passed through a room of readers at wide tables. In a corner bookshelf filled with leather-bound books, he pulled out a volume and began to page through the handwritten lists.

"Bergmann, Paul," he pointed.

Die Lyrik des älteren deutschen Sozialismus, "The Poetry of Early German Socialism," confirmed Paul's socialist commitments, though the topic suggested that his psychoanalysis with Isakower had softened the terms of Paul's zeal, giving him a more aesthetic and ethical approach. The dissertation had been accepted in 1931, by which time it was getting a little late to wax poetic about revolution in Austria. Though the socialists were still part of the republic's coalition government, and some of the social reforms that had made Red Vienna internationally famous were still ongoing, rising unemployment was pushing many young men into the arms of the right-wing *Heimwehr,* and Viennese spoke fearfully of civil war.

Back at his desk, the young librarian instructed me to fill out a card and return in the early afternoon, by which time the dissertation would have been brought up from the closed stacks. Though I balked at the delay, I was also grateful for the couple of hours to prepare myself for seeing what my father at twenty-five had produced.

Outside, the air was unusually mild and the sun was out. Having purchased a slice of pizza down in the Schottentor station, I walked across the trolley tracks into the Freud Park, where I sat overlooking the darkened gingerbread spires of the old Votive church. Students were taking advantage of the exceptional October day to play Frisbee and read on the grass. But the noon sun, combined with the pizza, added nausea to my apprehension. Actually, some form of unsteadiness arose with each new document that promised to reveal my father. Always uneasy about transgressing his strict silence, I feared another punishing discovery, at the same time as I hoped each time to find him again, at last. And so my nausea was partly the result of a wish so strong that it seemed capable of making him appear—just over there, in his loose jacket and pants, walking meditatively across the park!

As I re-entered the cool university halls around two, my heart was beating loudly, and I almost expected to be detained as an intruder. Yet I found my way unobstructed through the hidden passages to the library. The dissertation should have appeared in the alphabetized reserve slots under B for Bergmann. When it wasn't there, I looked under A for my last name, then sat down at a long table among the students and tried to calm myself by reading a newspaper. The librarians had changed for the afternoon shift. An hour passed, and no dissertation was visible under A or B. Finally, I asked for help from a new librarian, who after a few minutes' search found the misfiled volume.

Inside the dark cloth cover, the uncannily familiar typeface on the onion-skin pages brought back the portable Olympia my father had used throughout my childhood. A small black manual typewriter, ornately decorated with gold, it had special keys for the umlaut vowels, and the Z and the V were not in the positions I was taught to expect in my high school typing class. Although my father often promised to have the typewriter reconfigured for English, he must have resisted the change, for the little Olympia still had its umlaut keys and letters placed in the German order when he died.

Computers and a lavish use of paper have over the last decades created the possibility for flawless copy in all professional papers, and so the cross-outs and blue inked changes on the dissertation were initially shocking. Yet even as I felt a little embarrassed for my father, I was grateful to be able to see the corrections, for Paul's fine feathery hand gave an eerie intimacy to every page. I could imagine his slow methodical movements as he bent over the manuscript at his desk; his irritation—a sucking of the teeth—at catching a typing error; the effort of will he needed to refrain from inserting a belated insight, and so only strengthened a point with the insertion of an adjective.

I had been given permission to copy the dissertation, and never have I felt so careful and patient as I laid page after page, like a nurse smoothing the sheets of a sickbed, on the face of the library's very slow coin-fed machine. I remembered the day in 1974 when I defended my own dissertation at Columbia University. (Pre-computers, a professional typist had retyped the page whenever I made a change.) The war in Vietnam had only recently ended, and several academic departments had come under attack for their participation in U.S. military research. My field was anthropology, but I had gone against custom and done fieldwork in the most ordinary of American institutions, a public high school. My choice had been casually defiant, and I had accused myself of lacking the courage for the exotic studies that had turned Malinowski, Firth or Evans-Pritchard into classics. But these great texts from the era of exploration were being attacked for having supported England's imperialist adventures. "Study ourselves!" said the activists whose indignation held me captive.

My research had consisted of spending more than a year observing classrooms, school assemblies, and teachers' meetings; also leisure talk in the teachers' lounge and the students' lunchroom, and even the daily gossip at the mirrors of the girls' bathrooms. Though I knew my political sympathies were my father's, during all this time, I had never thought of my work as connected to his training as a psychoanalytic pedagogue. Having written my dissertation with methodical efficiency, I was one of the first in my group of graduate students to undergo the ordeal of the defense. Perhaps because my father was not alive to recognize (or belittle) my achievement, the handshakes of my professors at the end of that arduous ritual gave me little joy. Perhaps, too, I had ensured that I would have little to celebrate, for I had shielded myself from both my father's unachievable standards and my fear of competing with him by viewing anthropology as outlandish and taking a cynical, deprecating attitude toward my study of an American high school.

READING MY FATHER'S dissertation was supposed to have taken up a few lonely evenings in Vienna. I'd thought of it as a good way to pass the time inside my rented room, when no engagement drew me back out into the night. But beyond the poor lamplight Mrs. V. had supplied, and the patchy quality of my father's typing, I came upon enough German words I didn't know that, without resorting to my dictionary, I was losing much of the meaning.

Besides, life both inside and outside the apartment was destabilizing my careful habits. One late afternoon I returned to find Mrs. V.'s large unopened suitcases with their Aerolineas Argentinas tags filling the corridor. They remained there for several days, while she sat at the phone, once again installed in the hall, loudly reconnecting with her Viennese friends. I began to come upon her in the morning at her open bedroom door, an aging Brunhilde, brushing her long, thick, salt-and-pepper hair and then twisting it into a loose luxurious bun. Each time she returned from shopping, the refrigerator filled with meats and packaged cheeses, and the narrow kitchen workspace became more cluttered with fruit and onions and loaves of bread sliced open and going stale.

Luckily, I was beginning to have my own social life, and was less reliant on the refuge my room had once supplied. A lunch with an American journalist during my first week in Vienna had turned into a pleasant weekly tête-á-tête while sampling the city's famous old restaurants. And one Saturday, I had taken an early train to Semmering, the mountain village whose "exaggerated comforts" young

Paul had traded for Mariazelle in 1917, and where nearly a decade later an older Paul had recuperated in a tuberculosis sanitarium. After wandering for several hours on a trail along a high mountain ridge, I had met a biologist my age, Christine, hiking with her retired laboratory assistant, Walter.

Curious about my search for my Viennese father, Christine devised social evenings in which I could share my latest discoveries. Since Walter, who was a little older than we, had learned the old Gothic German script in school, he helped me decipher the official documents while Christine made Viennese dumplings in her narrow apartment kitchen.

After dinner, I curled up on one of Christine's small couches, and the three of us talked about what growing up in Austria and America had been like. Although I had resisted my mother's pity for the suffering of the ordinary "Aryans" who had remained in Austria or Germany, I saw that my mother had been right about the hardships families like Christine's or Walter's had faced during the war and its aftermath. Like other refugee families in America, we had the anxieties of dislocation, and we lived frugally long after my father's earnings might have given us some ease; but we had never suffered hunger and malnutrition, as they had. We were rebuilding our lives in the United States when Christine's and Walter's families were still trying to stay clear of a murderous regime; and our nights were restful when they were huddled in basements with the sound of bombers overhead, only to return in the morning to homes that had lost a roof or a wall.

In April 1938, the Austrian Nazi government passed a law demanding that all civil service employees show proof of having four Aryan grandparents. Directed mainly to "cleansing" all government positions, including the public schools, of Jews like my father, the law had wider effects. In Christine's case, the man who would be her father had been illegitimate, and though he had appealed to his biological father to vouch for his heredity, Christine's grandfather had feared exposure to his wife and family. By the time Christine was born, her father was an unemployed "non-Aryan." Even after 1945, her father remained a beaten man, unable to rebuild his career. Fifty years later, Christine could still break into a raw fury at the racial laws that had disgraced her father and forced mine to flee. Courageous in her own life, she hated her biological grandfather's cowardice and mourned her father's inability to rise from defeat.

IT WOULD BE more than two years later that, dictionary at hand, I would read the self-assured, analytical, erudite prose of Paul's dissertation—and what pleasure, what surprising joy, it would give me!

Die Lyrik des älteren deutschen Sozialismus examines the poetry that flowered in Germany and the German-speaking areas of the Habsburg Empire in the years leading up to the revolution of 1848, when Jews like Paul's grandfather were still forbidden travel to the great capitals. The poetry of Georg Herweigh, the son of a poor Stuttgart innkeeper; Ferdinand Freiligarth, a banker, and Heinrich Heine, a Jew who spent much of his adult life in exile in France, would become classics, loved by all readers of German literature. A few poets would have a narrower but fiercely loyal audience among socialists in the First Austrian Republic. But most would remain unknown names or appear as "anonymous" in the ephemeral newspapers that arose in the wake of the revolution and at best were compiled in little anthologies of socialist or revolutionary poetry that lay in dusty archives at the time Paul was working on his dissertation.

Paul's story of the flowering of socialist poetry in 1848 showed an easy, often joyful synthesis of politics and literature that must have been increasingly difficult to maintain as the Austrian Republic succumbed to fascist dictatorship and then to Nazi occupation. I would glimpse my father's political and literary confidence in the 1950s, when he brought home a library copy of Upton Sinclair's *Arrowsmith* and other classics he considered essential to my moral development. But in the American heartland, his aesthetic opinions seemed merely another instance of his unreachable majesty. I had never fully appreciated the intellectual comfort he must have had in German literature, the tradition he both revered and felt entitled to criticize. Reading the manuscript, I could sense the handsome, articulate young teacher he had been: intellectually gifted, politically democratic, approachable on those days he wasn't in a bad mood, and perhaps more magnanimous than he would be with his own children, whom he could never forgive for being Americans and girls.

Still, Paul's apparent identification with the anguish of Heinrich Heine's life as a Jew took me by surprise. Characterizing Heine in exile as carrying his Judaism as "sickness, his Germanness as pressure and longing," Paul argued that Heine and other Jews were often in the forefront of revolutionary and liberal movements *exactly* because, living under ever-changing restrictions on Jews, the benefits of full citizenship were so obvious to them.

Respectful of those who used their pens to support the revolution, Paul also showed humility about his limits as an intellectual. After a short poem, *Brandraketen,* "Fire Rockets," which commands readers to take up their arms, not their pens, *"und nehmt euch selber Brod und Recht,"* and seize for yourselves bread and rights, Paul commented, "The invitation, not to seize the pen, as an introduction to a six-line poem is somewhat funny." He was also critical of bad poetry, some of which he quoted. But I recognized his self-lacerating insistence that aesthetic judgement must take second place to building a more just world. "The laughter about aesthetics dies at the thought that one might dare turn away from the tragedy of millions expressed in the mouth of one of these millions."

MY FATHER'S POLITICAL views were muffled by the pall with which the McCarthy years covered the Midwest, and so came to me indirectly, in sardonic comments and oblique wishes. By contrast with the parents of some of my New York friends, who had well-worn copies of *Das Kapital* in their bookcases, argued about the Soviet Union over dinner, and sung the *Internationale* at holiday parties, my father's idealism was wrapped in bitter loss and longing, transformed into a whipping block for his own lonely integrity.

I was sometimes aware that injustice didn't worry my midwestern classmates, but I never thought to adopt their happy innocence. Disquiet with the uneven parcels of the world's bounty was as deep in me as being a Jew. Even my mother, without the philosophical scaffolding of socialism or the communal liturgy of Judaism, assumed common cause with the have-nots and the prejudiced against. In my secular family, these were the rational, self-protective, and honorable choices.

One summer afternoon, my father was visited by an old Viennese friend who had immigrated to the Soviet Union around the time of Hitler's invasion of Austria. The deep lines of her sharp face showed intolerable disappointment, and when she opened her mouth a row of aluminum teeth was a frightening testimony to Soviet dentistry. But I don't think the betrayal of her hopes made my father more forgiving of capitalism as it played out in his home in exile, or made me take seriously the dark side of the socialist dream.

THOUGH VIENNA AS a city was conservative, generally polite, and often elegant, my final ten days in Mrs. V.'s apartment seemed to bring an ever-increasing breakdown in manners and civility. One afternoon, as I opened the crowded refrigerator, a large uncovered bowl of kidney stew fell out, and soupy dark brown globules splashed across the kitchen floor. I grabbed a spoon and a sponge and was on my knees when Mrs. V. entered the kitchen.

"Please get out," she demanded from high above me.

Mortified, I went to my room. A couple of hours later, I took my remaining few items from her refrigerator and stored them on my windowsill. From then on, I used the kitchen only early in the morning to boil water and pour it through the decaffeinated coffee I had brought from New York. Then I quickly returned to my room to have my solitary breakfast in the little sitting area.

Yet minimizing my reasons to use other rooms in the apartment was not sufficient, for my own room was no longer inviolate. One afternoon, I came home to find Yuri, emboldened by Mrs. V.'s return, seated at the grand piano. Having opened the hood to maximize sound, as if for a concert audience, he was in full throat of a dramatic piano sonata. My carefully photocopied pages of *Das Lyrik des älteren deutschen Socialismus,* which had been in a tidy pile on the piano hood, lay scattered on the floor.

"*Heraus!* Get out!"

"Shh! . . ." he nodded to the accelerating passion of his performance.

"*Heraus!*"

Furious, I went over to the piano and grabbed his shoulder.

Banging the keys, he suddenly stood up. "You are the most cold-hearted Jew I've ever met," he hissed, scooping up his music.

As he sashayed out of the room, he turned back for a moment. "I wouldn't tell Mrs. V., if I were you!"

I picked up the pages of my father's dissertation. With Mrs. V.'s return, the tenuous bond between Yuri and me had been severed by the favors and secrets Yuri and she now traded, often casting an eye on me to see whether I had observed their cozy intimacy.

From then on, I avoided socializing in the hall and kept my bedroom door locked. Though I assumed I was still being called to the telephone when someone rang for me, I felt I had strayed onto a minefield I only vaguely understood.

1 3

Café Prückel

A COLD OCTOBER SUN SHONE on the wet-leafed pavement in front of Café Prückel at the edge of the Stadtpark, where I stood waiting for Thomas Aichhorn on a blustery Saturday afternoon after a morning of intermittent rain. Behind the sheer white curtains of the high-ceilinged café, Viennese were leisurely sipping coffee while they read newspapers strung on bamboo poles. Unsure of the direction from which Aichhorn's grandson would be coming, I looked back toward the narrow curved streets of the Inner City, then down the leafy boulevard, shimmering copper in the October sun.

In December 1936, August Aichhorn sent a photo postcard of himself to Semmering, where Paul was recuperating from a bout of tuberculosis. A wide-cheeked older man, wearing a dark fur-collared winter coat and wide-brimmed hat, looks straight out from the photo. Famous for dressing only in black, Aichhorn is supposed to have cut a dashing figure, but the small mouth draped by a long, white, handlebar mustache and a narrow white goatee seemed a little comic to contemporary eyes. The son of a baker, Aichhorn had worked with other boys in the bakery, and had begun his career as a teacher in a vocational school. Believing that he might easily have become a delinquent, he had successfully directed Ober-Hollabrunn,

August Aichhorn in a photo postcard he sent to Paul in Semmering

which treated particularly aggressive adolescents. By the mid-1920s, having undergone analysis with Freud, he was assuming a certain authority among both Viennese educational bureaucrats and maverick Jewish psychoanalysts. Like Siegfried Bernfeld, Aichhorn pioneered antiauthoritarian and democratic methods of working with youth. But, while Bernfeld had placed his hopes on building a new society of youth in Palestine, Aichhorn sought "reconciliation" between working-class adolescents and their Austrian authorities.

"Frau Ascher?"

A man with a pleasant boyish face and graying hair was suddenly before me. He gave a quick Austrian bow.

"*Guten Tag.*"

We made our way past the low-hanging chandelier in the elegant pale mustard room to a window booth of knobby wool in the same musty color. A few awkward minutes while we wrestled out of our trench coats, perused the menu, and ordered; then steaming cups of strong coffee were placed before us.

On the phone, Thomas Aichhorn had remarked that, although he had his grandfather's files, the name Paul Bergmann was entirely new to him, and I had felt the familiar sting of sorrow and chagrin as I again feared my father's marginality. Then, seizing the cold comforts of a researcher, I had written down general questions about psychoanalytic pedagogy that I hoped Aichhorn would be able to answer.

A careful man, whose reverence for his grandfather's experience easily matched mine for my father's, he had gone through August Aichhorn's papers in preparation for our meeting. Now he set before me copies of several published articles that Paul had sent Aichhorn after 1945, when correspondence was again permitted between the Allied and Axis powers. My father had spoken as if he had cut all ties to Vienna. But the articles showed that, over the years, he had quietly sent his work to his old Viennese teacher. And, of course, the photo postcard of August Aichhorn had been among the few items Paul had taken with him in late 1938, and it had remained in his closeted packet of photos through our numerous moves in the United States.

"I know my grandfather mourned terribly the loss of his friends," said Thomas, who made clear his own regrets—his grandfather had died when he was only five, and he had constructed a mentoring grandfather largely from other people's memories. "He often complained that the most dedicated had gone, the brightest had gone. He had lived in a world of progressive Jews, and the Nazis stripped his world from him."

Among the articles Thomas Aichhorn had copied was a spoof Paul had written in Topeka in 1948 for August Aichhorn's seventieth birthday festschrift, *Searchlights on Delinquency*.[16] After a short introduction in which Paul referred to his own work with delinquents in

Vienna and hoped that his jest gave tribute to what Aichhorn had taught him, the article proceeded as an imagined speech to a meeting of gangsters. According to the tongue-in-cheek argument, society's theories of criminal behavior, rather than being objective, were bent by the moral high ground which social prestige and power accorded to "honest men." The implicit critique was characteristic of my father, for whom honest men were never far from being scoundrels, and those who invent theories of criminal behavior were as interested in enhancing their careers as in changing the attitudes of criminals or, more difficult, finding ways to make antisocial behavior unnecessary.

The festschrift's table of contents lay between us on the café table, as Aichhorn, the grandson, mulled over it with me. Anna Freud, Willi Hoffer, Paul Federn, Kurt Eissler, Fritz Redl, Paul himself—I could see most of the contributors sitting in our Topeka living room in the late 1940s. Still living in Vienna ten years earlier, they had written their essays in England and the United States. What scrambling and hardship had filled the intervening decade for both Aichhorn and his former associates! And how painful, if also reassuring, it must have been for Aichhorn to receive a book in his honor by analysts whose rebuilt lives in distant continents he could hardly imagine.

I looked up from the festschrift to meet Thomas Aichhorn's flirtatious blue eyes. His warmth seemed to welcome whatever I might say. But, knowing he was an analyst made me afraid of revealing the flood of childhood memories evoked by the festschrift. Instead, I put aside my prepared questions, and, taking cues from the psychoanalytic method, held back and listened.

It proved a good strategy. As he smoked one cigarette after another, Aichhorn reminisced on his own life and his grandfather's heritage. Like August, Thomas spent part of the week treating working-class patients at a city clinic. For some years, he had also wanted to write about the efforts of his grandfather, Anna Freud, and Siegfried Bernfeld to build a psychoanalytic pedagogy during the inter-war years. The trouble was, he thought, we both had delayed too long. Most of the refugees who had been part of the movement had died, and the remaining few were growing too old to be reliable informants. As a less ambitious project, Thomas was arranging the letters between August Aichhorn and Anna Freud in the years after the war, when August tried unsuccessfully to lure her back to Vienna.

Why hadn't August Aichhorn left Vienna? I wanted to know. Not surprisingly, there were overlapping explanations. Most clear was that August's son, Thomas's father, who had worked on the plebiscite for Austrian autonomy, was arrested and shipped to Dachau on March 13, 1938, the day Hitler marched across the border. Gaining his son's release from the concentration camp was August's overriding reason for remaining in Vienna after the Psychoanalytic Society was closed and his Jewish students and colleagues said their anxious goodbyes. (Of the sixty-eight members of the Vienna Psychoanalytic Society in March 1938, only Aichhorn and two others would still be in Vienna in 1945, when the city was liberated by the Allied powers.) Aichhorn's son was released from Dachau in the fall of 1938, but the young man remained under Gestapo surveillance. Other personal reasons also prevented August Aichhorn from leaving Vienna, including a longstanding liaison that made it difficult to leave with either his wife or his mistress.

Over the next seven years, August Aichhorn put his political and psychological cunning to good use as he kept psychoanalysis alive. In September 1938, the Vienna Psychoanalytic Society was transformed into a Viennese outpost of the German Reich Institute, and the emphasis shifted to genetics, eugenics and other racially-motivated research. While Aichhorn covered his tracks by becoming a nominal member of the German Reich Institute, he continued quietly to analyze patients in his own home, to offer psychoanalytic training, and to hold seminars on psychoanalysis, using editions of Freud he smuggled in from Hungary.

In 1946, Aichhorn and the fourteen young analysts he had trained during the Nazi occupation reopened the Vienna Psychoanalytic Society, and he became its new head. Then in 1949, after a year of illness and recovery, Aichhorn suddenly died. He was just over seventy years old.[17] The catastrophe of the Third Reich—not only for those who had perished or managed to flee, but for Austrians like himself, who had survived through blindness, subterfuge, and compromise—had finally caught up with him.

It was dark outside the café window when Thomas Aichhorn suddenly looked at his watch. He had promised to baby-sit his granddaughter—until this moment, it had completely slipped his mind! Would I please excuse him? He sprang up and gave me a solemn bow. Then, with a cigarette between his lips, he hurried out of the cafe.

Alone at my table, I became aware that the leisurely afternoon coffee drinkers, reading under their table lamps, had given way to an early dinner crowd. I sat a while longer, making notes on our meeting. I still knew little more than that Aichhorn had trained Paul to use psychoanalytic techniques with "wayward youth," and that Paul had used this training to work with delinquents. (Thomas Aichhorn had looked through his grandfather's files to find out where, but had been unsuccessful.) Still, it made a new kind of sense that in Topeka Paul had visited Southard School each week to work with the delinquent boys there. I also had a better sense of the shrewd and inventive man who had become an important mentor and teacher to Paul. The same age as Paul's father, Aichhorn had likely matched Eduard's skill at accommodation and diplomacy, while bettering my grandfather at holding onto his unique vision. Knowing how easily my father could be hurt, irritated, or judgemental, I suspected that Aichhorn had been the one to make the gestures of conciliation— even agreeing with a warm smile to the frustration his own tolerance and compromise evoked in his young Jewish colleague and friend. It would likely have benefited me and my sisters, had Aichhorn still been in our father's life when we were growing up.

Throughout my meeting with Thomas Aichhorn, I had spoken only German, and I had spoken it on my father's once mysterious psychoanalytic terrain. I knew that my *Deutsch* had been accented and my sentences Americanized; but rather than humiliation for not sounding like a native, what I felt was pleasure and a sly pride at my fluency and daring.

It was past five when I left the café and made my way in the cold dark evening toward the commercial lights of Landstrasse and my rented room.

AFTER MY FATHER died in 1965, my world turned dangerous as kitchen knives, gas flames on stoves, and the hot surface of an iron all seemed to trap me. When I walked through a plate glass window, filling my knees with shattered glass, I knew I could no longer trust myself and made my way to a public clinic to find a therapist. It was a year after his death, and I was twenty-five. Psychoanalysis itself had blossomed into countless sects and tendencies over the half century since Paul, at twenty, had walked over to Pelikangasse to apply to the Psychoanalytic Institute. A handful of warring groups all counted themselves as the "true inheritors of Freud," and there were Kleinian, Adlerian, and Reichian analysts, as well as Gestalt, client-centered, bioenergetic, and dozens of other therapies that saw Freud and his followers at best as distant inspirations.

Yet, like everyone hoping for relief and release, my own venture into therapy was uncertain, and my desire to become stronger and less self-defeating was equaled by a wish to cling to the capricious, disarming father whose judgments and demands still shaped my life. In truth, the cutting and burning was a warning of the extent to which I was ready to go in the hope of being reunited with him.

ON FEBRUARY 12, 1934, two weeks after Paul's twenty-eighth birthday, the Schutzbund, the military wing of the Social Democratic Party, precipitated a brief but bloody civil war in Linz that ended the fragile Austrian Republic and brought Paul's dreams of building a rational and just society to a violent end. In Vienna, some hours to the east, Chancellor Dollfus was hearing mass as the lights went out in Stefanskirche. He didn't know until later that the streetcars had also stopped, which was the signal for a twelve-hour strike that was to inaugurate the insurrection. But the Schutzbundlers' plan to take over the Inner City was badly conceived. Combat between Schutzbundlers and the police actually began in the outer districts. Otto Bauer and other social democratic leaders, who had hoped to avoid armed struggle, escaped to Prague once the fighting began. Leaderless, the outlawed and weakened Schutzbund was no match for the Heimwehr, the police, and Dollfus's new army.

Though the fighting dragged on for days, the insurrection soon turned into a defense of the workers' housing complexes built by the socialist city government over the past decade. Constructed with inner courts to create workers' communities, these buildings became fortresses that one by one fell to Dollfus's artillery. The Karl Marx Hof, the great kilometer-long housing complex that had become the pride of social democracy, was the last to fall to heavy machine-gun fire, on February fifteenth.

Three days after the Karl Marx Hof had surrendered to military bombardment, Paul again visited the Kultusgemeinde. "*Rucktritt, 19 Februar, 1934*," read the penned notation, marking his return to Judaism after ten years.

It was unlikely that he had grown fonder of the tribe and rituals of his parents, but my father had a principled courage. He must have told himself grimly that he had miscalculated. With an incendiary mix of Catholicism and fascism transforming Austria, it made no sense to make a personal declaration for the victory of science and reason. Since Hitler was making a Jew a matter of genes, my father would stand with his race.

1 4

Herta's Story

I N THE POLICE STATION THAT second day in Vienna, I had met a tall, muscular young man with thick dark hair framing a well-chiseled face. Having graduated from a technical school in his native Tyrol (which was why he needed to keep his Viennese residence form up-to-date), Klaus was working in a Viennese sporting goods shop. But some of his friends were public school teachers in Vienna, and he was eager to know where my father had taught school. Over the next weeks, Klaus called fairly regularly to hear what I was discovering. Since he had told me that I was the first Jew he had ever met, I was uncomfortable about what my heritage might mean to him. Anyway, I was busy with new discoveries, and I held him off each time he offered to help me with my research. Yet I kept delaying my visit to Vienna's Stadtschulrat, the central educational authority.

When just over a week remained of my stay in Vienna, Klaus called to tell me that he knew exactly which department at the Stadtschulrat held the records of all public school teachers. He had also arranged his day off to accompany me there.

Situated at the outer edge of the Ring, the Stadtschulrat is a beautiful cream-colored building whose grand stairways and wide pale halls encircle a large inner atrium. I hung back as Klaus requested

directions with excessive Viennese courtesy. After two or three efforts, we found the correct department, but were directed to sit on the
white wooden bench in the hallway until told to enter. Carrying files,
people hurried by with an inwardness and urgency I had never seen
at New York City's Board of Education, where any errand is also a
chance to pause and chat. Although I was glad for Klaus's company,
his tone had suggested awe of school officials and uncertainty about
the reception that a Jewish research project would receive.

Finally, a door opened and we were instructed to go into an inner
room, where a bald, burly man sat behind a vast mahogany desk.
As he listened to Klaus, he got up genially and turned to the shelf
behind him. A row of annual books recorded all Viennese *Gymnasium* teachers by the districts in which they taught. A number of
books were dated between 1910 and the early 1920s, when Paul
would still have been a student. Then, after a hiatus, the books re-
sumed in the 1940s. Only one book coincided with my father's career in the public school system: it was 1937-38, the school year that
ended prematurely for all Jewish teachers.

The archivist held the book as we went district by district in
search of Paul Bergmann; by the last page, we had found two
schools in different outlying districts in which he was listed as a
Hilfslehrer, or teaching assistant. Although the entries recorded his
teaching certificate from 1929 and reaffirmed his Ph.D. in 1931,
being a Jew had apparently kept him in two part-time jobs at the
lowest professional rung.

While the pages were given to an assistant for copying, the
archivist explained that one of the schools where Paul had taught
was temporarily housed in a boat in the Danube, and it would be
next to impossible to get old records there. But the Bundes-Gymnasium Nr. 54 in the Sixteenth District was open. He and Klaus discussed the best streetcar to take, and he gave me his card and told
me to use his name.

Klaus was anxious that his day off be used to complete my
school research. Pleased by our easy success and the kindly face of

a Viennese bureaucrat, he hurried me onto a streetcar headed for the outlying district.

A half hour later, we jumped off the streetcar to face an austere white-plastered three-story building. Inside the school, the spacious halls were decorated with Mondrian-like mosaics, fashionable in the 1950's when post-war repairs were likely made to the structure. The headmaster, a gaunt stringy-necked man in a three-piece suit, was standing in the middle of the main office. When Klaus mentioned that we were seeking records for a teacher who had worked in the *Gymnasium* until the spring of 1938, the headmaster turned away abruptly and busied himself with papers. It took a minute or two before I grasped that he was actually pretending we were no longer there. Klaus stood next to me, immobilized. This was the humiliation from which he had believed his presence would protect me; he hadn't imagined that his very request, uttered with friendly Tyrolean respect, might turn him into a pariah.

Unwilling to be blocked by the headmaster, I approached a gray-haired woman with a kind face, seated at a nearby desk. Giving me an understanding nod, she brought out a hand-written log from the 1930s. The left side of the page listed the courses the school had offered; on the right side, next to their subjects, the teachers had signed their names. Under *Deutsche Sprache*, German language, I recognized my father's delicate fluid signature.

The ledger book listed the twenty-six girls in Paul's class, along with their birth dates, religions (two were *Hebräisch* and one *Konfessionslos*), and the grades—*gut* or *sehr gut*—he had given them. It was odd to see my father so generous with praise, when we, his daughters, had so rarely merited a *gut*. It made me wonder, whether, as a Jew, he had felt obliged to inflate the grades of his Catholic students, and whether this, in turn, had fed his antipathy toward praise.

Now, with a copy of the page at my side, I see a pattern I didn't notice at Bundes-Gymnasium Nr. 54 that day. Of the school's twelve teachers in 1937-38, five, including Paul, must have been unable to prove that all four of their grandparents were Aryan. Teachers of

German, philosophy, mathematics, gym, and choir—like Christine's father, they had all been let go on April 20, 1938, and their Aryan replacements had penned in their signatures above the signatures of those dismissed. My father's class had been taken over by a Dr. Erwin Schenck. Though the book didn't record the student transfers, the three "non-Aryan" girls would surely have been kicked out in April along with their Jewish and other non-Aryan teachers.

Klaus had stood by quietly while I read and copied the pages. As we left the school, he kept going over the moment the headmaster had turned away, as if somewhere in the cracks of what we had both witnessed might lie another interpretation of the man's rude behavior. He also needed reassurance that I had recovered and didn't blame all Austrians for the prejudice of one small-minded man.

HERTA LENG WAS a former Viennese *Gymnasium* teacher whom my father had taken our family to visit in Troy, New York. As I began to reconstruct Paul's life, I had found her phone number in the Troy telephone book and driven up to see her. Herta recalled that she and Paul had lost their teaching jobs the same day. A notice had been placed in the box of every Jew in every Viennese school. That was it. They had to assume that an Aryan teacher was moving their students forward. Paul, who was already seeing a few children privately on Werdertorgasse, plunged into more psychoanalytic work. But Herta was stunned. She knew how to conduct theoretical research and teach physics; if these professions were banned to her, what was her career? Then, amazingly, she was called to teach physics in a *Gymnasium* that had been unable to find an Aryan replacement. She was barely adjusted to her students in the new school when she again received notice, though soon after a third school needed her to teach math. It seemed for a while that she would survive the racial cleansing—so long as she could agree to the cold dismissals and was willing to be an itinerant teacher in whatever corner of math and physics temporarily lacked Aryan expertise. But finally, of course, the public school system had solved its staffing problems and she received no more calls.

Sitting in her tailored living room chair, her thin legs set squarely before her, there was a stiff grace to Herta's solitude. Twenty years after retiring from Rensselaer Polytechnic Institute, the latest issue of the *American Journal of Physics* lay on her coffee table, a magnifying glass holding her place. Though it was a hot July day in upstate New York, shade from the front porch gave her darkened living room a cool timelessness.

Herta's cautious story of her relationship with Paul paid respect to my mother and guarded her own privacy. She had met him, she said, while accompanying a friend who was visiting him in a sanitarium. She no longer recalled exactly what had been wrong with him, most likely tuberculosis. It was so common in those years of unheated houses and inadequate food. In any case, Paul soon returned to Vienna, which was when they began to see each other regularly.

What had drawn her to him were the glimpses he gave of the hidden layers of the human mind and how understanding these layers could make her life easier. Before meeting him, she had assumed that it was her responsibility as a teacher to deliver a sequence of scientific information, and her girls' responsibility to leave their excitements and concerns outside class. While Paul was respectful of her physics research, he helped her understand the psychology of her students, and made her rethink how students learned. She had never heard a teacher, and certainly not a man, speak with such insight about young people.

Did she know about his work with juvenile delinquents? I asked. Only that he counseled them, and that it seemed to enrich his teaching. Herta recognized the name Aichhorn, but she had never met the man. Inside the tightening noose, where they were each trying to survive along with their aging parents, the world she and Paul came to share was quite private.

"It was the fascist period leading up to Hitler and our emigration," she said quietly. "But we were often very happy together."

She had rented an apartment, an unusual solution for a young woman, but she and her mother didn't get along. This was something else she spoke to Paul about. And, although her apartment was tiny, it held a piano on which she and Paul often played pieces for four hands.

On a hunch, I asked Herta about a brown cable knit cardigan my father had worn throughout my childhood. Knit by "a friend in Vienna," it grew ragged over the years. Yet he clung to the warm sweater, periodically bringing it to my mother to re-sew the seams or patch an elbow. "I was thinking after you said you would drive up from New York that I had knit him something. But I wasn't sure, was it socks? Was it a sweater?" Herta smiled, her delicate face momentarily lit by intense feeling.

Careful not to mention my mother's repairs, I told her only that my father had worn the sweater long after the wool began to shred.

"*Ja, ja, ja,* it was I who knit it." She was nodding, her lower lip now turned with sadness. She was a modest reclusive woman, seemingly overwhelmed by unspoken emotion. But she knew how to steady her rudder, no less at momentary pride in her unusual intellectual accomplishments than at the more tenacious emotions of disappointment and grief.

HERTA HAD BEEN talking for a long time, and I worried that she had come to the end of her strength and needed a rest. But she wanted to look for an old photograph album she thought was in the top drawer of her bedroom chest. I followed her into the bedroom with its carefully made narrow bed and stood at a distance as she rummaged through her drawers. Tucked in the pages of a red leather album were photos she had secretly taken of Austrian soldiers with machine guns, patrolling empty streets during the 1934 civil war. She paused briefly to study them with me. But they weren't what she was searching for. Finally she found the photo she had remembered: it was a close-up of Paul, his long hair slicked back from his face, his eyes dark patches, as he aimed a cold smile at the camera. The smile brought to mind the disdain for danger I sometimes see in the broad smiles of black men in New York. Though I had witnessed my father's rage on countless occasions, I had never seen that brazen icy smile.

My father had told a story of saving himself and a friend, but the details had been vague, evaporating each time I tried to hold them steady. Long after his death, as I began reading about Vienna in those first months after the *Anschluss,* I encountered any number of unbearable scenes that gave witness to the Nazis' sadistic imagination: Jews being forced to write "*Judisches Geschäft. Kauft nicht bei mir ein!*" (Jewish business. Don't buy from me!) on their own store windows. Jewish women made to don their best fur coats and then clean the cobblestones with their own toothbrushes. An old Jew's beard set on fire, while Nazis watched casually, promising to shoot him if he tried to put out the flames. But nothing I read solidified the fleeting image my father had left with me.

"You and my father were almost trapped by the Nazis, weren't you?"

She nodded. They had been out walking when they entered a square. A group of Jews were being demeaned, while the Nazis stood together in a knot, laughing at their tableau.

Starting to slow down, she heard Paul's tense instruction: "Keep walking until we near them. Then laugh." He took her hand, and walked toward the scene. As they passed the Nazis, they both stopped, as if transfixed, and laughed long and heartily.

"You don't recall what the Nazis were doing to the Jews?"

Whether she was protecting me from an intolerable memory, or had herself consigned it to oblivion, she couldn't go further with the story. What she wanted me to appreciate was his bravery and quick thinking in the face of such danger. It was his understanding of human psychology that had enabled them to survive. Having entered the square, Paul had seen that their only escape was to pretend that they were an Aryan couple out for a stroll, enjoying the spontaneous entertainment the Nazis were providing passersby.

Herta's shadowy story suggested that whatever I had heard from my father had also been muffled, even botched, which was why my memory of the story was never clear. What he *had* conveyed was his lingering shame. Perhaps his laughter at the tormented Jews in the square had evoked an earlier longing to escape his victimized heritage. Although he knew it made no sense to obey a genocidal regime, in the silent harshness of his self-judgment, his ingenious escape that afternoon must have come to seem a betrayal.

HERTA'S BROTHER IN Switzerland thought he might be able to help her and Paul leave, and Herta spent days preparing her papers for emigration. In the meantime, she was called to Gestapo headquarters to explain why communist literature was discovered in her mailbox. Though she knew her frosty demeanor didn't help her cause, she was immobilized by fear. Finally, a Nazi officer brushed his hand insinuatingly against her cheek, told her it was a pity to waste such beautiful blue eyes on a Jew, and sent her home.

Paul thought she should use her Zionist connections to get out of Austria. He had obtained a visa to Hawaii from a former patient at the Vienna Psychoanalytic Society, but he had to wait for his name to come up under the U.S. immigration quota. His cousin Trude and her new husband, Ernst Trebitsch, had turned over all their property, paid their "flight tax" and were on their way to Sydney, thanks to Trude's younger sister Lotte, who had had the foresight to emigrate a couple of years earlier. With Trude gone, Paul had suddenly rushed to the Chinese Embassy; but after a day of standing in line, he had not even gotten inside the gate.

Then Herta and Paul had a new scheme: they would offer themselves as a butler-maid duo to an English family, while they waited entry to the United States. Paul had studied English with his cousins before they left. Herta found a woman in the Ninth District to give them private English lessons, and they began to go there together nearly every day.

"Goot-mor-ning. It-iz-suje-nize-veaz-er."

Herta thought Paul's English exceptionally awkward and dull-witted. How could a man with perfect pitch, who had mastered Latin and French, make English sound like a Czech dialect?

"I hef alvays lofed Zayne Ghray. Alzo Zinklare Luvis."

But Paul said English sounded like the clacking of a typewriter. The prospect of hearing it all around him made him fear for his musical ear. To make clear his contempt for the capitalist robber barons and cowboys with whom—assuming any luck—he would one day share a barbarian future, he exaggerated his mistakes. Not that Paul had much love left for German culture, which had adapted so easily to maliciousness and brutality and mob rule. Sometimes he fell into a silent, angry despair, and Herta was afraid that he would lash out at her, and felt trapped in her own helplessness.

The day came when all Paul's papers were ready. Herta picked him up on Werdertorgasse, and was surprised by the shambles she found in the once carefully appointed apartment. The candelabras and silverware had been confiscated, Paul's books cleared from the cupboards. Even the carpets were rolled up. His parents were to be moved in with other Jews at a new address. Her own papers, as Herta had discovered on a second, more ominous visit to Gestapo headquarters, would be delayed until she confessed to the whereabouts of the friend for whom the Communist literature had been intended. The trouble was, her friend had probably either gone underground or left for the Soviet Union.

She stood quietly by while Paul said goodbye to his parents. It seemed unlikely that they would ever see each other again. Paul hated scenes, and his mother was sobbing. Herta had promised to accompany Paul to the Bahnhof. Gathering his knapsack and suitcase, they took the tram together through the streets of Vienna for the last time. Then, suddenly, she was alone on the platform, trying to wave bravely as Paul's train pulled away.

———

Lying in the narrow bed in Herta's guest bedroom in Troy, I scarcely slept as the night hours crept by. For a long while, I gazed beyond her dark yard at a light in the next house. My body seemed to rest an inch above the bed in a state of rapture and grief, whether for Herta or for my father, I wasn't sure. I had only felt like this before the start of a dangerous affair.

Herta had told me that she expected to be reunited with Paul in England, but that a few weeks later he wrote that he had a new woman. The romantic story of a refugee wedding, along with a photo of the

Herta Leng beside a cyclotron, soon after her immigration to the United States.

two in front of the English courthouse, was in one of the first news-papers she read a few days after she finally arrived from Vienna.

The light next door had finally gone out, and the night was an inky black, as it never is in Manhattan. Hurt and bruised on Herta's behalf, I wondered whether this very ordinary romantic betrayal was one of the many things for which my father had also lacerated himself. Yet, even in my own more comfortable life, I had experi-enced how passionate attraction, as much as fear, can wreak havoc with morals and reason. Being in free London, the romantic com-mitment Paul had formed in Nazi Vienna must have seemed in-fected by humiliation and fear.

Still, I couldn't help imagining myself as Herta's daughter, raised by a woman whose thoughts traveled in equations that encom-passed the far reaches of the universe. How different it would have been than with my own mother, who was left cold by the most modest speculation! Yet, just as I had been strengthened by my mother's optimism, my father must have been warmed and reas-sured by her sunny exuberance, which seemed capable of blocking the ambivalence and self-criticism and regret that had plagued him for most of his three decades. I could also see that Herta would have been a cooler, more ambitious, self-involved, and fretful mate and mother—someone more like Grandmother Antonie. And my father had loved my mother, at times with less self-protection and reserve than he would likely have been able to love Herta.

Herta's story made clear the source of Paul's abstract warning when I was a teenager that men didn't marry their intellectual equals. Yet, how much easier my own early adult choices might have been if, instead of his generalization about male desire, I had heard his own complicated and all too human story.

THE NEXT MORNING, sitting over the pretty breakfast table Herta had carefully laid for us, I asked her exactly what she and Paul had promised each other before he left Vienna.

"I was always the more emotional one," she answered sadly, deferentially, not wanting to implicate him.

Given how things had turned out, and the many long years in a new country during which she had mastered her grief, she may no longer have even been sure about his promises. Yet she said he had taken advantage of business trips several times over the years to visit her in Troy.

"Did he mention Mother and his family?"

"No, we didn't talk about such things. But I knew he was happy to be with me, and we were happy together."

Overwhelmed by a passionate grieving that was for myself as much as for her, I blurted, "I wish he had married you!"

"But if he had, you and I wouldn't be having this wonderful breakfast together." Herta smiled at me.

1 5

Eduard

I HAD TAKEN THE STREETCAR to the Zentralfriedhof cemetery at the southern edge of Vienna, near Schwechat Airport, the Saturday after my first talk with Frau Weiss. Having thought little about Eduard Bergmann, the long bus trip out to the cemetery visit seemed one of those gestures of sentiment that retroactively embarrass me. Knowing that I had altogether only five precious weeks in Vienna, I even accused myself of avoiding research leads by spending half a day to pay homage to a grandfather I had never known.

At the Catholic and Evangelical gates of the cemetery, weekend visitors were buying paper cones of hot roasted potatoes before they carried in the gardening tools and vases of flowers with which they would tend their loved ones' graves. The Jewish cemetery was the farthest south. But after walking south at the narrow edge of the road for ten minutes, I found the wrought iron gate to the Jewish section shut and locked. Locked. Unable to face a thwarted long journey, I buzzed and rang and buzzed again, with rising nausea and panic. Finally, a haggard-looking woman in a faded blue cotton worker's coat stuck her head out of the gatekeeper's house.

"*Shabbes! Es ist Shabbes,*" she called out in accented German.

"I want to visit my grandfather!" I shouted back. Hardly aware of what day it was, I had entirely forgotten the Jewish prohibition against polluting the holiness of the Sabbath by contact with death.

"*Shabbes, geschlossen!*" the woman called again, and disappeared.

I began crying helplessly. From what dark sea of misery had this come? For several minutes, I sat crumpled, succumbing to wracked sobs at the closed gate, while the cars whizzed by a few feet from my ears. Suddenly, three little boys peered at me from inside the gate. They must have thought I was the recent anguished widow of a much-loved partner. The oldest boy was trying to direct my attention to a sign on which the cemetery hours were posted. The face of six childish eyes made me seize control of myself. But all my crying and confused grief had made me hot, and I was pulling off my raincoat in preparation for the walk back to the streetcar, when an adolescent girl in a worn sweater appeared. Taking a heavy key from her pocket, she silently opened the gate for me.

Embarrassed at my unearned victory, I dug out the scrap of paper on which Frau Weiss had written my grandfather's grave number.

Silently, the girl led me along the paved main path, as lush with old overhanging trees as a European palace garden. The large upright marble and granite stones were decorated with signatures of the deceased, or with sentimental inscriptions like, "Gone but not forgotten," or "Death cannot break the bonds of love."

Alone in the cemetery, except for the occasional drone of a plane overhead, all was still.

"*Sie sind jugoslawische?*" I asked, after awhile.

"Bosnian."

Turning left, we neared the southern edge of the cemetery, where the trees were younger, scarcer, and the plots patchy and more worn. Now I noticed the flat cemetery stones of Jews who had been starved or gassed, and whose corpses had been destroyed, in the gravesites which held nobody: "In memoriam, deported . . ."; "In memoriam, to my beloved mother, killed in 1942"; "In memoriam, died September 1944, Auschwitz." We were within section 20a, which consisted of dozens of metal markers designating the graves of Jews who had died between October and December 1938, during the violent time surrounding *Kristallnacht*. Perhaps there had been no remaining relatives, or their relatives had been too impoverished or harassed, or in too much of a rush to leave Vienna, to see to their gravestones. These were my father's last months in Vienna, and the metal markers suggested a nightmarish world from which he had fled.

We were searching for 20a, row 1a, but could locate only row 1. Overcome by a new surge of sorrow, I wandered unsteadily, reading blurred numbers and names as I sought reasons why my grandfather might, after all, not be buried in the cemetery. A damp wind had come up, and I had put back on my raincoat. But the girl's sweater was too light to be out so long, and she was holding her thin arms across her chest. Feeling that I had extracted more special attention than I deserved, I pulled a 100 schilling note out of my purse and promised to come again the next day when the cemetery was open and someone was in the office.

We walked back along the tree-lined path of the closed cemetery, our silence matched by the stillness of the tombstones. The little boys had disappeared. The girl unlocked the gate to let me out.

WHEN PAUL HAD gone, the apartment on Werdertorgasse stood irrevocably empty in the blue winter light. Antonie and Eduard had moved into the apartment as a young couple when their son was two: slowly they had filled it with furniture, books, china, photographs and the piano he had mastered so beautifully. Even when he had been studying outside the city, taking a trip or recuperating in a sanitarium, they had known that his absence was temporary and he would soon return to them. Now Antonie fretted about Paul's safety during the long trip north through Germany on his way to England. What if he were pulled off the train and his papers found wanting? She had always sensed that under German efficiency lay heartlessness and cruelty.

But it was Eduard whose loss was inexpressible and who seemed to age overnight. His Paul! The boy on whom for nearly half his own life he had lavished all fatherly pride. Painfully, he remembered the beautiful baby who had become the talented, obstinate, sulky boy, and then the enraged and righteous youth, whose opinions had been too cleverly formed to argue against; yet, after troubling years of worrisome turns, Paul had become a handsome young man, gifted in a range of work Eduard didn't try to understand, and pleasing to an intellectual kind of woman Eduard had never dreamed of for himself. Eduard's heart stopped in sorrowing love when he passed the closed door to the now empty room where Paul had sat at his typewriter and seen his patients. With all that Eduard had been forced to sign away, it was Paul's departure that transformed what remained of his life into terrible futility. A Catholic neighbor, wearing the swastika band, had already stopped by to run his hands insinuatingly over the unused grand piano.

THE MORNING I discovered Eduard's military record in the State Archives, the clerk brought me an additional folder pertaining to my grandfather. Also in the old Gothic script, for Hitler had reinstated it for official records, the materials in the second folder documented the results of the April 1938 law, which made it illegal for Jews to own property, and so allowed for the confiscation of anything valuable owned by a Jew. The earliest of the forms had been filled out and signed by my grandfather on July 15, 1938, when Paul was still living at home. Like all Jewish males, Eduard had been assigned the middle name Israel. Asked to catalogue his holdings, Eduard Israel had carefully written: a sock and necktie factory, two outstanding loans, and several savings accounts, including one in Prague. Two months later, while Paul was still at home, Antonie's apartment building on the Wiednergürtel would be confiscated—the Aryanization papers for this transaction were also in the State Archives.

Eduard and Antonie had apparently leased their Werdertorgasse apartment, and I could only approximate the moment of their forced eviction—the result of another law forbidding Jews to live in the same building with Aryans. The new Kolschitzkygasse address, Number 14, Room 503, appeared for the first time on a legal paper signed in February 1939, two months after Paul's December departure for England. In this first document completed at the *Gruppenwohnung*, or "group home," Eduard Israel had been encouraged to list his remaining valuables in full detail, for he wrote that he still owned two large carpets, six small carpets, one watch and a wedding ring.

Several additional papers signed at Kolschitzkygasse were evidence of Eduard's and Antonie's attempts to get out of Austria in late 1939 and early 1940. In September 1939, Eduard was charged a *Reichsfluchtsteurer*, or departure tax, of just under 20,000 Reich Marks. This was said to be equivalent to one-fourth of his worth, but the already confiscated factory machines and inventory were included in the calculation. Eduard must have fought the tax as too high, for a month later a second, adjusted tax—this time called a *Sicherheitsbescheid*, a security payment—was set slightly lower, at 17,000 Reich Marks.

Though I had both accepted and fought my parents' feelings of luck—and guilt—for having escaped Europe, these documents made unbearable reading. As one tries to acclimatize oneself to scalding water, I would read the files in short bursts, at first with the help of Christina's friend, Walter, and later alone, until I could endure longer stretches of concentration. Beyond the forbidding German legal language and the Gothic print through which I felt the brutality of the Nazi regime, the documents shattered the highminded disdain for property that had been so useful to my parents, and that I had mindlessly inherited from them. I even saw how my father's socialist principles had likely rigidified as a defense against an untenable loss. So much had been taken from us—on my mother's side, as well as my father's!

I had gone to see my grandfather's factory in Penzing (it was now a mirror factory), as well as my grandmother's apartment building on the Wiednergürtel near the Südbahnhof. Standing before the buildings, I imagined them still being owned by our family. The thought didn't give me particular satisfaction. Like my parents, I took pride in having earned what I owned by my own wits and labor. Like them, I felt strong because I was neither fettered nor softened by inheritance. Yet, as I stood in front of the buildings, I could see that my own Spartan ethic was partly a defense against envy of those whose lives have been eased by inheritance.

The bulk of Eduard's file pertained to the "Aryanization" of his factory in Penzing. In December 1938, around the time of Paul's departure, a legal document authorized the disposal of the factory, as well as the appointment of an "Aryan interim administrator," Egon Josef Bauer, who was to take charge of the firm until its permanent Aryan owner was decided. A month later, in January 1939, a Dr. Hans Wagner spent a week at the factory at the expense of the Gestapo (his itemized bill was enclosed with the report), during which he conducted a thorough inventory of my grandfather's business. In addition to detailing eleven employees—three, including the foreman, were Jews—the inventory listed the machinery, the raw materials, and completed products (Dr. Wagner pronounced the socks of "medium quality"), and the firm's profit-and-loss statements. One of Egon Josef Bauer's first recorded acts was to eliminate the three Jewish workers, an act of racial cleansing that was also a cost-cutting measure, since the Jews were not replaced with Aryan workers.

The file contained a complaint from Eduard, who in a seemingly insane act of righteous courage argued that the factory was being offered at far below its value. There was no response. Among the most interesting correspondence in the file, however, were applications from six Aryans who in early January 1939 expressed interest in owning the sock and necktie factory. The application form asked the "race" of the prospective owner and his wife, his previous professional experience, his financial worth, what he was willing to pay, and whether he was a member of the Nazi party. Sensing the importance of correct beliefs, a Herr Kriplinger wrote that he had been a cell leader in the Austrian Nazi Party since 1932, and that, because of his militancy, he had even been arrested three times during the period when the Nazis were still illegal in Austria.

Despite the varied talents and fervent ideology of Herr Kriplinger and the other five applicants, Eduard's factory was given to a Herr Grois, another Nazi Party member who must have made his bid by the back door, for, although the legal transfer of property to him was included in the file, there was no evidence of his formal application for ownership.

THE DAY AFTER my first visit to the Zentralfriedhof, I took the second of what would be four streetcar trips out to the cemetery. It was Sunday and nearly noon when I arrived at the Jewish gate. Inside the office, a gaunt, once pretty woman in a short-sleeved white blouse was typing on her computer with one finger, while an elderly European couple looked on. When it was my turn, I presented my slip from the Kultusgemeinde.

The penalty for leaving Israel off the name of a Jew must have extended to the cemetery registry in 1940, for the computer listed my grandfather as Eduard Israel. The cause of his death was given as "unknown."

Marina, the attendant, had heard about my unsuccessful Saturday visit from her neighbor, who also worked in the cemetery; she herself was the mother of two of the little boys who had peered at me through the gate. As it was past noon, she closed the office and went outside with me to help find my grandfather's grave.

Oblivious to the niceties of grammar, Marina's truncated German had the slow, dull tones of a daily effort to fight dislocation and grief. Two years earlier, her husband had been killed in Croatia and their house destroyed. She had brought her boys to Vienna, and the cemetery job had been a bit of good fortune, since it came with a small apartment on the grounds. The Jewish visitors, who were patient when she misunderstood, had taught her a rudimentary German. Yet beyond the modest benefits of the cemetery job and the conversations that Jews like me provided, being surrounded by death and mourning must have enabled her dozens of times a day to perform her own private acts of mourning.

Near the southern edge of the cemetery, with the aid of a map Marina had brought along, we saw that row 1a was perpendicular to row 1. Eduard's grave, disguised by a buildup of wet leaves, was on a small path serving half a dozen unkempt and overgrown plots. Brushing the leaves from the large flat stone, we read:

Eduard Bergmann 1872–1940

The grave held the man who had fathered Paul, as he had fathered me. If Eduard could speak from his grave, as my father never had from his, what thoughts would he share? Lichen and moss clung to the pitted granite. I spent a few minutes trying to brush away debris and make the stone look tended. I would try to have the granite repaired.

IN JULY 1937, Paul and his parents took their last vacation together, at Altmünster, a mountain resort on the Trauensee. I know this from a final black-and-white photograph that shows them sitting at an outdoor table under the trees. Eduard looks overweight but genial in a light suit and tie as he squints at the camera. He has belted his slacks over his high paunch, and the hair around his bald pate is now white. Next to him Antonie, still dark-haired, has become matronly in an Austrian summer dirndl. (A year later, the national dress would be forbidden to Jewish women.) On the right, Paul is well-dressed in a white summer suit, but he seems to sit quite separately from his mother and father.

I try to fathom the intimacy and irritation, the compromises and denial among the three: an only son in his thirties and his aging hard-working parents. Each must be making worried plans. How much do Antonie and Eduard express of their anxieties? What does Paul tell his father, his mother? It is he, with his years of political and psychological reading, who must understand the propaganda and

The last photograph of my father with his parents, and the last photograph of Eduard.

terror that is building the stranglehold of fascism, and so takes the long pessimistic view, forecasts the worst.

It is pouring on my last Sunday in Vienna. For the fourth time, I have taken the streetcar out to the Zentralfriedhof, where I stood under my umbrella to view Eduard's newly refurbished gravestone and said goodbye to the grandfather I never knew. Now I am standing in the rain in front of the apartment building on Kolschitzkygasse, a working-class street a few blocks from the Südbahnhof where, starting in 1941, Jews would be herded onto trains headed east. I know the exact room—Number 503—where Eduard spent his last days, and where Antonie would live until her escape by train to Portugal, and from there by boat to the United States. But my heart is too heavy to get out of the rain and go up to the fifth floor.

What words could possibly explain the purpose of my visit?

I know that in the Kolschitzkygasse *Gruppenwohnungen*, a dozen families and their possessions were crowded into an apartment intended for a small family. I also know that after 1939, Jews were allowed in shops during only a few hours of the day, and food for Jews was strictly rationed. My grandmother wasn't the kind of woman to joke about the miseries of a tightening noose. If my grandfather attempted to normalize the situation with humor, his more serious effort at "normalcy" was to continue going to the factory for a year, though it was now under the direction of Egon Josef Bauer. But the records show that by 1940 Eduard was eased out completely. Left without work or income, he must have lived more in the past, taking a pained pleasure in sending old photographs to his new daughter-in-law in Hawaii.

One day, an envelope arrived from Hawaii with two tickets from Vienna by train across Russia to Vladivostok and from there by boat to Japan and on to the American continent. It was a trip my grandfather must have dreaded.

Suicide is strictly prohibited by Jewish law, and the records in neither the Kultusgemeinde nor the Jewish cemetery mark the many suicides of Viennese Jews during the Nazi years. Cause of death: unknown. Cause of death: heart attack, or arterial sclerosis. It was Heidi Weiss who had put that dark idea in my mind. Yet I didn't think Eduard had taken a pill or put a gun to his head. He was a man of sixty-eight, living on bad food and no exercise; he had suffered round after round of disillusion, humiliation, and plunder—my research had surely revealed only the tip of what he had suffered. Drawing on his military experience at Wieselburg, Eduard must have understood why the *Gruppenwohnung* was located so conveniently near the trains.

Antonie would have found his cold body. Alone, she would have decided not to leave Vienna with the tickets her son had sent, but to buy the granite gravestone and give Eduard a proper burial. She was a methodical woman, her bravery easily obscured by propriety and complaint.

Safe in Topeka, she would sing me songs like *"Ach, du lieber Augustin"* and *"Du, du liegst mir am Herzen!"* that she remembered from Vienna—songs whose simple melodies and sentimental lyrics seemed pregnant with a pain I did not know how to ask about.

In 1946, my father wrote an article on child development in

which he argued that, through rational discussion, parents should "inoculate" their children against such adult tragedies as war.[18] But he himself could speak about Vienna only in ponderous generalities, or in off-handed ridicule at veterans who had believed that there would be a place for Jewish patriots in Hitler's Austria.

And then, in 1952, still in Topeka, Paul published an essay on "Music in the Thinking of Great Philosophers."[19] An odd article for a former German literature teacher or a psychoanalyst whose tools are words, it used Socrates' decision in *Phaedro* to compose hymns as he awaits his death to argue that there are experiences, inexpressible by language, which can only be communicated by music.

Yet it is *Deutsch*, with its inexpressible pain, that even now can suddenly waylay me with love for him.

IT IS TEN-THIRTY in the morning, the last day of October. Although it is a little early to leave for the Schwechat airport, I have finished packing and there is nothing more to do in my rented room. Yuri is in his room with the door closed, and I don't feel like knocking to say goodbye. My suitcase is loaded with my laptop, portable printer, and the many documents I have copied; my big knapsack, packed with clothing, is on my back, and a small pack, also stuffed, hangs over one shoulder. I have gone down the stairs once with the packs, and I am dragging down the suitcase, when Mrs. V. suddenly looms at the door.

"Just one thing, rather negative, on which we all agreed," she calls down. "Yuri, the cleaning woman, and I, we all thought that your coffee smelled terrible."

Balancing my suitcase, I look back at her, stunned. Why is she telling me this now? Though I know I should let her have the last word, my voice cracks as I say, "I'm sure you'll have great fun talking about me, the three of you, now that I'm gone."

"Oh no," she laughs. "There's nothing else. Just the coffee. We all agreed, it smells like thirty percent malt, thirty percent shit, and I'm not sure about the last third."

I don't know how to answer; I have already said too much, for her voice seems to be gathering a joyful energy.

"Thirty percent malt, thirty percent shit . . . !"

"I stopped cooking, coffee was all I made in the last two weeks," I hear the sob in my voice. I am remembering the kidneys and suckling pig she ate with her fingers, directly out of encrusted frying pans. Only once had I talked to her about my research. It was after I had met a woman, a Viennese Jew, who had attempted to return to her old home after the war. "Those Jews don't belong here anymore," Mrs. V. had said, as if I were telling a story about yesterday. Down at the bottom of the stairs, I hitch my knapsack onto my back and my little pack onto a shoulder. Perhaps it was my caution and control she hated.

She is still laughing. "Really, we were worried, Yuri, the cleaning woman and I. It couldn't be good for you, a coffee with such a stench."

"I'm sorry," I say, the fury making me tremble. "I just wish you had told me a little earlier, if it bothered you so much." I turn my suitcase and begin to drag it out the door, through the courtyard, and out to the street, where I will catch a bus for Schwechat Airport.

I am still trembling with fury as I miss the first bus, then twenty minutes later catch the next one, and the trembling continues as the bus speeds along the Danube toward the airport. Only yesterday, busy with the last of my research and saying goodbye to Walter and Christina and Thomas and his wife, Friedl, all of whom have become new friends, I had regretted leaving my father's city. Now I can't wait to get out of Vienna.

In the airport, I'm still trying to regain my balance. But I keep hearing, "You smelled, you smelled, oh, the stench." Mrs. V., the Jew in hiding, the convert, the daughter of a Nazi? I know only that she is supposedly a native of Vienna, whose family now lives in Argentina. Somehow she has managed to condemn me. Hearing her reverberating words, I have rediscovered that raw place of tribal victimization. Have I somehow been party to this ghastly exodus?

16

Werdertorgasse Again

I N THE FALL OF 1996, MY HUSBAND Bob and I were staying in Vienna with Thomas Aichhorn and Friedl Früh—the recent bond had already become strong. As I continued to piece together my father's past, there were archival details I needed to check, and I still hadn't been inside my father's apartment on Werdertorgasse. Ten years earlier, when the stumbling old woman had led us to my father's street, Vienna had been mysterious, threatening. Now, the encounter with Mrs. V. had faded into an inexplicable oddity, and I was jumping onto streetcars, and sharing familiar cafés with Bob. Vienna had become a beautiful, complicated city, with its peculiar range of humanity.

Although I was determined to visit my father's apartment, the prospect unnerved me. As we turned onto Werdertorgasse, no amount of talking to myself calmed me and I was blinded by a migraine headache. For the moment, just as ten years earlier, I let Bob take charge.

At Number 9, the sign of the Socialist Party was still on the building. Adjacent to the dry goods shop, now owned by a Herr Wiener, Bob pushed open the large front door. A cavernous unheated area might once have garaged two carriages or cars, but it was empty except for several bicycles. The stairs were of stone, wide and airy, with decorative floral wrought iron railings.

"I think we should go up," Bob said.

On the *Hochparterre*, the hall floor was still mosaic, as it must have been during the Bergmanns' years. The sign on the smoky glass *Jugendstil* front door announced the office of an apartment renovation firm; we rang the bell and were buzzed in.

"My father lived in this building from 1910 until 1938 . . ." I began, as a woman came smiling to greet us.

"*Ach! Eine schlimme Zeit!*" A terrible period! she said, looking distressed, and offered us coffee, which we declined. What I *did* want, I said, was to walk around her office, as well as to look out the window, to get a sense of the house in which my father had lived for most of his first thirty-three years.

Opening a couple of doors, she told us to go where we wished, and returned to her papers. The firm was in the business of showing the possibilities for modernizing: new narrow slatted wood floors had been installed in several rooms; a gleaming white kitchen boasted the latest in streamlined appliances; and subtle lighting fixtures brought a contemporary warmth and cheeriness to the rooms. Still, the sixteen-foot ceilings were there, as were some of the wide old floorboards. I could mentally furnish the living room with the dark ornate furniture, delicate china, and Oriental rugs my grandmother had cherished, and with Paul's grand piano. The glass doors, which were original and beautifully carved, had led to the bedrooms, Paul's filled with a typewriter, books and papers and, in later years, an analytic couch; his parents' with the comforting heavy bed and wardrobes of aspiring Viennese Jews.

I could also imagine the Bergmanns' apartment as it had last stood, largely emptied, unprotected.

I went to a long high front window and hung out my head. It was growing dusk, as I surveyed the Bergmanns' dim narrow view. When I leaned far out the window, I could glimpse the edge of the Danube Canal beyond the end of the street.

My father must have hung his head out like this, as a boy, as a youth, as a young man, to watch for a friend, or to judge the weather. And on that day of exile in late 1938, as Herta waited by the door, Paul probably stood at this window and looked out one last time, taking a silent mental imprint of the view down to the narrow street below to hold in his memory like a hardening stone, gathering the silent sedimentations of sorrow and temptation and longing to return.

1 7

Peterborough

I T WAS LATE MAY, MORE THAN three decades since our father's death, and we were making the long drive from New York City to Peterborough, New Hampshire, to visit his grave. This had been my sister Miriam's idea, and her strength of will and resourcefulness had been evident as she persisted with her plan during the winter months. She gave me alternate dates for joining me in New York and sent me the flight numbers of possible airplanes she could take. As the time drew near, she flooded me with anxious phone calls: Would I rent the car in New York? Did I want her to get an AAA Trip-tik? Would we stay in a motel one night or two? Although I have learned to proceed as if I believe in a benign and trustworthy world, Miriam's anxieties unearthed the doubts and suspicions I struggle to keep at bay. When I told her I didn't want so many telephone calls, anxious letters in her large, stiff, shaky hand awaited me in my mailbox for the next several days. In any case, visiting our father's grave together was something I also wanted to do. The plan was coming to pass.

I had gone alone to see his grave in 1979, shortly after I changed my last name to Ascher. In a frenzy of mourning, I wandered around the rural cemetery, unable to find the grave, then stumbled onto the small flat stone under a stand of pines at the edge of the road. Getting out my shovel, I had planted a dazzling purple azalea. Did the lush violet effusion betray my undiminished yearning, despite my efforts at gaining distance with a new name? Guilt and embarrassment surged alongside my grief, as I drove away in a blur of tears.

The years since then had not diminished the possessiveness of my sorrow. Each time I told friends about going to New Hampshire, I spoke of visiting "my father's grave." Then, catching myself, I promised to master the plural by the time Miriam arrived in New York to join me on the pilgrimage.

Throughout the late winter, as Miriam made her anxious preparations, Mother advised against going whenever she and I talked on the phone. Although she claimed that the grave was merely the *place* where her husband was buried, and so unimportant to her, she insisted that Miriam wasn't strong enough to see it. As usual, Miriam's weakness and her own strength arose naturally in the same sentence, as if one hinged on the other. I began to wonder if Miriam would fall apart in some new way while we stood at the grave.

We spoke of this, Miriam and I, as we drove north through the acid green of the late burgeoning spring. She could see how Mother's determination to view her life as lucky, despite the loss of her country and culture and her early widowhood, had atrophied the darker end of her emotional range. Miriam herself often got caught in uselessly demanding that Mother own up to worry or grief. But she also confessed to the fear Mother had attributed to her. She was afraid she would "see him" in the cemetery. What exactly did she mean? I was aware once again of her stiff language and anxious stutter: she pushed against a thicket of interference, starting and stopping several times within a phrase, and repeated her last words each time before going on.

"Well, that he will ... that he will ... will suddenly be there."

She made me see him as huge as life, rising to meet her. The Zeus-father we had both feared and adored, demanding and fury-ridden, without his moments of humor and exquisite gentleness. Above a woolen shirt or winter coat would be his large head, his jowls sagging, his eyes judging her from behind his glasses, as he walked slowly, ponderously, toward her.

I glanced at Miriam, who was gazing out the window at the rolling farmland. She had been a beautiful child with light blond curls and huge blue eyes. But the curls had darkened and turned frizzy in puberty, and she must have been in her thirties when she began to gray. Now her kinky hair, obediently dyed on the advice of a job counselor who was seeking to lessen her reliance on disability insurance, was held away from her face by a bright magenta head-band; but the hair color she had chosen was mahogany; brown hair made her skin sallow and sharpened the anger and grief on her face. As if in rebuttal of her cautious speech, the whole of her ceaseless inner turmoil erupted in rapid changes of extreme expression, at times accompanied by grimaces and tics.

"Anita says this trip will make me feel closer to Daddy," Miriam said, her brow hanging darkly over her wary eyes.

I had not heard of Anita, but realized that she must be the latest in a succession of psychotherapists whom MediCal allowed Miriam to see in treatment for a maximum of twenty sessions.

Until our father's death, she had been a frail, awkward, skinny child, who was often too fearful to eat even the foods she liked. They had been on a camping trip in the White Mountains—Miriam and our parents—that August when he succumbed to his fatal heart attack. Suddenly she ate as if her stomach sent no signal of being full, and she gulped down huge quantities of liquid: soda, juice, sweetened coffee, ice water. As we drove north, she remembered the moment when her attitude toward food changed.

"Mother gave me an orange that afternoon when we came back from the hospital in Peterborough, after Daddy died. We were lying on the motel bed, and as I was eating it, I thought: yesterday I would have been too afraid to eat this orange."

She then used the word "relaxed" to describe why she could now eat the fruit. Relaxed seemed odd for such a shattering moment, yet plausible and poignant. If the discipline of psychoanalysis had given our father a certain professional distance with Miriam, it had not blunted his paternal disappointment and impatience, and his voice had too often boomed with disgust and rage. "Miriam, you cannot go without any lunch!" Sometimes, as she knelt beside his blue chair for help, her purple mimeographed exercise sheet aslant on her lap, he suddenly yelled, "*What?* How can thirteen divided by forty be ...!" and slammed his fist against the arm of his chair. "Don't you ever think?" His wrath, which stung and paralyzed me, must have thrown her into a primitive convulsion, for she never developed the coquettish charm with which to regain his warmth, and she had refused to develop a clever skill by which to distinguish herself as his talented daughter.

"Daddy hated it that I couldn't tell him what I was thinking, like you and Barbara did," she had confessed earlier, making me see my self-exploration as bait with which I had snagged his affection. Yet knowing the humiliation of my self-exposures, I had secretly cheered Miriam's odd courage as she stubbornly remained silent throughout week after week of visits to a child psychotherapist. How much more resistant she had seemed than I!

But did she really mean "relaxed"? I asked, imagining her next to Mother on a cheap motel bedspread of quilted flowers, stunned by grief, as they waited for Barbara and me and our recent husbands to find our way to Peterborough. Yes, she answered. Ever since our father's first heart attack when she was five, she had been afraid that he would die. But after the catastrophe had finally happened she was no longer afraid, she could let down her guard.

I didn't question her further, but remembered how soon after our father's death she began to thicken around the waist. She continued to gain weight during her twenties and thirties, turning lumpy and leaden. She looked bulky and asexual, in aggressive defiance of the tanned athletic bodies that formed the ideal in the Southern California shopping malls near her home. Over the last decade, as she lost a series of ever less demanding jobs, her regimen of psychotropic drugs grew from year to year, until she finally went on disability insurance. While her cheap t-shirts rode up, her elastic-waist polyester slacks slipped below the overhang of her belly, exposing a strip of flesh in which she appeared to have lost all interest. Her watchband dug into her swollen wrist, and her fingers, which had once been long and delicate, were awkward and puffy. Even her attempts at grooming could seem provocative and unbalanced, as when she had appeared for dinner at Barbara's house with depilatory over her lip, because, as she blandly explained, she knew Barbara disliked her facial hairs, but, only remembering to apply the white paste at the last moment, she hadn't had time to remove it.

Yet over the past half year, Miriam had eagerly conveyed the latest good news of her SlimFast diet each time we talked on the phone. By eating the packaged blueberry cookies two meals a day, she had lost eight, then fifteen, and then over thirty pounds. In the car, she interpreted her new ability to sustain such discipline: having stopped menstruating, she no longer needed to protect herself from men. (Did menopause make her feel less subject to male sexual interest, or had her own desire waned? I wondered, but didn't ask.) Although she was still too heavy for her slight frame, she no longer had that deadened bloated look, and she moved more rapidly, her gait less defiant and fearful.

I had been disappointed too often to hope for a belated miracle; still, there were additional changes. She was making herself liked as a volunteer reader to children in her local library. She was taking care of her dog, handling his sieges of fleas with a certain maternal equanimity. After a conversation in which she confessed to being afraid of death, she had quickly followed up on my suggestion to join a synagogue—an act of outreach which showed particular bravery in the face of our mother's dismissive bewilderment at any expression of spiritual longing.

I began to ask Miriam about our father's death, at first to relieve our silence and so pass the time more easily as I drove. She had been there that summer night in the camping ground. I had not. From that silent swirl of sorrow, anxiety, and rage, Miriam's memory could emerge laser sharp: she remembered their hike his last morning in the mountains, and my father's decision that afternoon not to drive into town to shop with her and Mother, but to stay at the campsite and work on a lecture he was preparing for a conference in New Orleans.

"So he had no idea he was going to die," I said, wondering quietly if that also meant he thought he had time to reconcile with me.

Miriam also recalled the man in the campsite to whom she and Mother had handed over the family's black terrier, when they drove my father down the mountain in the back of the station wagon to meet the ambulance waiting on the highway. She herself had resisted getting into the ambulance with him, so someone else from the campsite had taken her in the station wagon, as they continued toward the hospital.

"Mamontek. That was it. Carol, do you want—do you want to see it while we are in Peterborough?" she asked, the sudden apprehension in her voice conveying her certainty that I would say no.

"Yes," I said, although something in her prediction of failure to achieve her wish made it a little harder to want for myself.

"THAT LAST YEAR, he used to cry in the morning while he shaved," Miriam tells me in the car. "You remember my room on Hampton Lane: my bed was against the wall next to the bathroom. I could hear him cry almost every morning."

I see her front bedroom, its Venetian blinds drawn; behind her room is a long modern bathroom with a counter of salmon tiles that my mother always intended to replace. My father soaps his brush and lathers his face as he walks meditatively back and forth. Thoughts of the day he faces—private patients, a meeting with his research team—come interlaced with the discontinuities of his life, his immense but shifting ambitions and spotty accomplishments, his rash idealism that still aches for the clarity of his Viennese youth. As for the knowledge and values he has tried to hand on to his daughters, they have proven untranslatable, useless, the daughters immersed in their American lives. And there is Carol. How he has found himself in such a dead end with her, he doesn't know. But his rage whenever his thoughts alight on her is such that he sees no way out. Suddenly he puts down the shaving brush, as the sounds of lonely remorse issue in clots from his throat. Miriam would have just awoken on the other side of the wall. With her tendency to paranoia and exaggeration, has she elaborated an isolated event?

Then, from the depths of something like remembering, I hear a man's sob, low-pitched, almost guttural, like choking.

THE CLEAR LATE afternoon light was casting bluish shadows on the cultivated rolling hills as we saw our first small sign for Peterborough. We put on sweaters so that we could keep the windows open and smell the sharp air. It wasn't even six o'clock—there were still a couple of hours before dark.

I had made a reservation at a bed and breakfast in Jaffrey, a town that the map showed to be ten miles beyond Peterborough. We planned to go straight there, then drive to the grave in the morning. The exact sequencing of our pilgrimage had been an ongoing afternoon theme, allowing us to express our anxieties even as it brought comfort to our silence. Mother wanted us to leave flowers in her name, so we needed to stop by a florist first. Yet I kept passing up florists and nurseries on the road, and the last one already seemed closed. Also, since breakfast at the B&B was likely to be elaborate, it would be nice if we somehow had the cemetery behind us—weren't dreading the visit. Yet if we went there too early in the morning, no florist would be open. Miriam now thought it would be good to drive directly to the cemetery even before going to the B&B.

"Carol, can we . . . can we . . ." she began nervously. We could go again in the morning, after we bought the flowers. But that way the worst would be over, we would be able to sleep.

She remembered that August morning at the hospital. While it was still dark, she sat in the waiting room, listening to our father cry out for morphine in the emergency room. She didn't want to be in there with him. They were massaging his heart—that's what Mother said when she joined Miriam for a moment. But they couldn't even give him morphine until a doctor came. Finally, dawn broke and the doctor was there; our father had been given oxygen and maybe morphine, because he was suddenly quiet as she saw him being wheeled away to a private room. She really didn't want to look. Mother was off to make new arrangements for a bedside nurse. Miriam went outdoors for air. Inside the hospital was the rush of medical people in white uniforms; inside was disaster waiting to happen.

She was standing by the station wagon when mother finally came out.

"She came over to me and put her arm on my shoulder and said, 'Daddy just died.'"

As Miriam's voice cracked, my eyes filled with tears. "I freaked," she croaked, her face collapsed in her hands as she heaved horrible sobs. I was trying to see the road through my own wet eyes, but suddenly she sat up and looked out of the window. "Why! Why, did I make Mother take care of me?"

"You mean, when her husband had just died?"

"Yes."

"You always have to be weak, so she can be strong." I'd put it too harshly; I could have reminded her that she was a fifteen-year-old, whose own father had died.

Nodding, she sank back into her memories. "Mother said, 'The doctor is going to come out soon to talk to us.' So we waited there in the parking lot, and after a while the doctor came out, and he said, 'Mrs. Bergman, Miriam, I just want to tell you that we did everything we could to save him.'"

"That's what he wanted to tell you?" I laughed. "That's what he came out to say?"

Miriam giggled; it seemed so absurd to us both, and for a while we both laughed convulsively.

When Miriam was still job hunting, I sometimes made suggestions, only to discover later that my "pressure" had upset her so much that she had telephoned her local hot line. As we reached the Peterborough city limits, Mother's worry about the cemetery visit began to nag at me.

""You know, we'll both be sad, standing at Daddy's grave," I said. "I don't want to have to ignore my own complicated grieving to take care of you."

She was silent a moment. "You didn't have to tell me that," she answered, hurt.

MIRIAM'S STORY OF our father's death had been a corrective, making me realize how in my mental pictures I stand at the center of our family dramas. While our relationship, my father's and mine, was the one that had imploded, I had left home my freshman year of college, six years before his death. The bedroom closet Barbara and I once shared had long been emptied of my clothes. While Barbara was the oldest daughter in the house for three years, she came home only for holidays and emergencies the last three years of his life. On a daily level, Miriam and my father and mother had constituted the family.

Miriam had told me about our father's second heart attack that year I was living in Spain. She was fourteen, and she and our father were supposed to have a couple of days alone while Mother paid a rare visit to Barbara, who was a junior in college in New York. But Miriam had been visiting a neighbor, and so hadn't heard the phone ring as he called from work again and again earlier that day. Her first indication that something was wrong was when she returned home and Mother suddenly opened the door.

Miriam also remembered Barbara coming home from college with a young man during the night, but she didn't mention a detail I had heard from Barbara: that Miriam had greeted her sister and her future brother-in-law with a baby bottle in her mouth. Actually, the bottle wasn't a detail I would have expected her to share.

Over the last decades, if I had erred in holding Miriam to standards of adult demeanor and responsibility she couldn't always meet, she and I had also shaped an environment in which she could proudly present her stronger side. True, I got a sense of her crazy states from Barbara, whose irritated insistence that Miriam could shape up, if only she tried, provoked her worst excesses. Still, when Miriam wanted my help or didn't know how weird she might seem, I glimpsed the nightmare that could constitute her private world. I knew the way she could manipulate others with thoughtfulness and courtesies in behalf of her own dependency, but I also knew her genuine kindness and childlike generosity, as well as her heroic attempts year after year to contain her bizarre side, to approximate her sense of what adulthood entailed.

As for my father, he kept to himself what he thought was wrong with Miriam, and perhaps his opinions changed as he observed her over the years. To us, he emphasized her cognitive difficulties, the trouble she had keeping up in school. Once he told me that a photograph had revealed damage to her brain.

On our Peterborough trip, Miriam told me that she hadn't wanted to see our father in the hospital after his second heart attack in Bethesda. It had been the same with his first heart attack in Seattle when she was five, but ten years later he and Mother insisted that she visit him nearly every day. I didn't understand why she resisted going: wouldn't she have been reassured by seeing him alive? No, she was too frightened to see him in an oxygen tent. I asked if she was afraid he would die before her eyes. She didn't know. Even after years of psychotherapy, she had little access to understanding her fears. I didn't ask her if she had believed that it was she—her illness, her handicaps, even her rage—who was killing him. Perhaps she had wished him dead: certainly, his rejection and disapproval had given her cause for terrifying hate.

As we drove through the soft New England farmland, the trees were still gray, their branches barely showing the tiny red buds that promise new leaves. Miriam recalled bitterly that our father had believed her incapable of even finishing high school. He and Mother were planning to send her to a vocational boarding school, where she would have learned sewing—that's what Mother told her after he was dead, and there was no longer the money for a special educational program. Yet after his death, she had struggled through junior college, and transferred to American University, where she had eventually graduated. Still, unlike Barbara and me, she had lived at home as a student, rather than in a dormitory. "He wouldn't have allowed that," she reminded me, her voice still conveying the sting of his judgment. Later, before what I saw as her breakdown, she had bravely moved alone to a different city to study for a graduate certificate in medical records management.

Miriam's belief that medical records management would give her a sense of professional dignity was deeply entwined with our family story. My father had regretted being a lay analyst, someone who had come to psychoanalysis from the humanities, rather than medicine. I myself began college as a pre-medical student, and dropped chemistry in a panic at an off-hand comment by a family friend that I must have an Oedipus complex and want to outdo my father. Some years later, while I was writing a commissioned book about women in medicine, I went so far as to write for medical school applications—only to back off amidst a surge of revulsion and fear. Although Barbara had cautiously chosen to become a psychological counselor (that is, to follow my father's footsteps, though with less training), her ambitions for her husband's career had been evidenced in strong direction and support, and he had become a physician. For Miriam, working with medical records meant partaking of this awesome world around which our family had circled. In addition, she could read about symptoms and treatments without directly witnessing illnesses; remaining within the hospital, fixated on the emergency room, she was as close as possible to the parking lot. Miriam had still been clinging to that poignant mix of professional and personal gratification when she began the mental tumble that had ended in her being certified as unable to work.

ALTHOUGH PETERBOROUGH FELT familiar, near the red brick mu-
nicipal building I let Miriam get out of the car to ask directions to
the cemetery. When she climbed back in, she directed me down the
hill to a small bridge where we took a left. As we passed the black-
framed windows of the funeral home, both of us felt a wave of
recognition. Until that instant, I had forgotten its pale flowered wall-
paper, as if a living room papered decades earlier had been converted into a funeral parlor merely by removing all furnishings but
the chairs. In the center of the room in an open casket lay our father
in a suit and white shirt. Miriam told me that Mother had mistak-
enly agreed to an "open coffin"—she was always for simplicity and
disclosure. She hadn't understood the expression and had been hor-
rified when she saw him lying there.

We had stood in a fragile little circle: Mother, Barbara, me, our
two husbands. Uncle Gerhard and Aunt Edith had appeared to
join our mourning party, as had my father's friend, John Kafka, a
psychoanalyst from Austria, along with his wife Marion. My
mother didn't want religion or ceremony; after living with my
father for twenty-five years, this was a matter of principle with
her. We stood quietly a few moments; then each of us stepped forward to say goodbye. Like Miriam, who had remained cowering in
the next room, my grief was suddenly overwhelmed by terror. I
dreaded my turn, dreaded touching him in death. But, unlike
Miriam, I knew that I would never forgive myself if I avoided this
one last contact.

When my turn came, I advanced to the coffin. His strong, well-
shaped hands, which I had always loved, were resting quietly at his
side. But the dappled beard he had grown while I was in Spain made
his lips sinister, marble-like. Through my tears, I kissed his pale forehead, so smooth and cold it was almost greasy.

Over the last months, his refusal to speak to me had deepened
my depression, which had emerged as a side effect of hepatitis.

Though his death had ended the anguish of his deliberate rejection, it had also extended his silence into all eternity. Standing at the coffin, I was momentarily furious at his leaving me in this terrible way. Then, overwhelmed by sobs, the pain of love seemed to swallow my rage. Moments later, it was over, and, quietly weeping, we got into cars and drove to the cemetery.

I had driven to New Hampshire to visit the cemetery only once in the three decades since his death, but I somehow knew to turn right and drive up the hill. I skipped the main cemetery entrance and continued upward. I remembered farmland on the right side of the road, but tract houses now stood beyond the stone fence. At the crest of the hill was a smaller entrance with a little sign posting the cemetery hours. I turned in, took the left fork so that I was going back above the road, and stopped by the pines.

The grave was flat and small, so inconspicuous in the pine needles and tufts of grass that one could almost walk over it without noticing. My father had wanted to be cremated. This decision, no different than his others, must have issued from a complex mix of anger and reason: his contempt for Judaic law, which demands that Jews be buried, probably combined with an insistence that the Nazi crematoria not influence his concern with population growth and the rational use of the earth's limited space. But in August of 1965, Mother had quickly decided that it made no sense to ship him to a distant cremation facility, when he could be buried in the White Mountains, which were so like the Alps. So her decision had also stemmed from a mix of motives: economics, expedience, and a tribute to his love for the terrain of his native Austria.

"I have always been angry at Mother for going against what Daddy wanted," Miriam said quietly. "But I see now, the cemetery is really nice."

I nodded. Yet the plot seemed too close to the sounds of cars shifting gears to make it up the hill. My father, as sensitive to sound as I, would have hated that noise, which must have worsened each year. But I was giving him life in death, as Miriam had.

The stone was far enough under the pines that it must have stood in shade most of the day; there were no shrubs nearby, not the azalea I had planted years ago, nor the birch Miriam said had been brought by a family friend, nor even a small bush that Barbara's husband had left the previous year when visiting the grave with their son. Miriam had seen a sign by the road indicating that only cut flowers were permitted, which explained the removal of our plants.

We stood at the grave another minute, relieved that no final emotional confrontation was demanded of us since we would be returning in the morning.

I WAS THIRTY-FIVE when I realized that I had the right to shape my own life, irrespective of either my father's wishes or his evaluation of my gifts. The major symbol of this change was deciding to write; this was less a matter of beginning the activity of writing than of taking the courage to send out my work and to call myself a writer. One could even, as it turned out, use the word "writer" on a tax form. Nevertheless, each rejection of an essay or story took on the ominous weight of my father's reverence for Art as something lofty, male—unachievable by a woman sitting at a desk. For several years, a warm-hearted therapist tried to convince me to give up the quest for my father's approval, which had done me no good. All evidence showed that he had never had either the generosity or the hope to applaud a child, his blood, a daughter. Yet giving up on him altogether was surprisingly hard. Rather than turning my back on him, I began to dwell on the love of intellectual and artistic endeavor that he had handed down to me, and to remember those moments in which my father comforted me and filled me with delight.

Miriam hadn't had my luck, in part because she so rarely had evoked his pleasure. Together, she and he had constructed a treadmill of disappointment, failure and illness, of knowing that she could grip his attention by provoking his anger or worry. Although our mother sometimes seemed to leap with pleasure to help

Miriam out, this had only solidified her stance as an invalid, some-one with severe handicaps.

When I climbed out of my four-poster at six-thirty the next morning, I parted the gauze curtains to find a sloping meadow bathed in drizzly gray light. Downstairs, Miriam was helping herself to a mug of coffee from the silver urn on the breakfront. Other early risers were seated at tastefully set tables. Miriam had told the pro-prietress that we were driving over to Peterborough and would be back before the breakfast service ended at nine-thirty. Yesterday, Miriam had been too anxious to drive, but now that we were on minor country roads and she knew what we would encounter, she wanted to try her hand at the wheel.

As she buckled herself into the driver's seat, she asked apprehen-sively, "Carol, shall we see the parking lot?"

"Yes, I thought we agreed that we would first go to the hospital."

Confidently, Miriam turned right toward the cemetery, though for her it was the route toward the Monadnock Hospital. We were on the steep two-lane road, passing the entrance by my father's grave, which she didn't seem aware of, but suddenly she veered into the left lane and began driving on the wrong side of the road. The oncoming truck leaned on his horn as he swerved to avoid a colli-sion and passed us on our right.

"Miriam!" I screamed, as she turned back into the right lane.

My heart continued pounding. Though I forbore interpreting her erratic death wish, my instinct was to get into the driver's seat. Still, I told myself that we had passed the dangerous spot, and I let her drive.

Chastened, she drove slowly through a wooded area and finally swung left into the hospital's long grassy entrance. Monadnock Community Hospital had more than doubled in size in the inter-vening years, as had the parking area, and the emergency entrance was now part of a new, modern-style wing.

Getting out, Miriam showed me the section that had existed that summer of 1965, and like detectives revisiting the scene of the crime, we paced out the old parking lot, noted where the family station wagon had stood, and took photos of the old red brick New England-style building with the white trim.

By eight, we were back in town, and when the nursery opened Miriam took the lead in buying deep blue cornflowers to leave in Mother's name. Jews don't leave flowers on graves, but that wouldn't have daunted Mother, and our father lies buried in a Christian cemetery. Back up the hill that was becoming as familiar as our own street, we made a left into the cemetery. Now we were standing before our father's grave again, this time in utmost seriousness, because we didn't know how many years it would be before we returned.

Miriam split the cornflowers and lay them diagonally, forming a blue roof over the top of the stone, while I hunted for little stones to leave as signs of our remembering. She hadn't known that Jews marked their graveside visits with stones. Pleased, she helped me choose extra stones for Barbara and Mother. We lay all four in a row under his name.

I had turned away with wet eyes when I heard Miriam calling into the grave: "Daddy, I'm not working now ..." She was crying, her words garbled by tears. "You wouldn't recognize me."

How grievous death is! How much suffering our father had left behind! We had each tried to make our own way over the past three decades, yet his death had hobbled each of us differently, leaving no one unscarred. I remembered my moments of angry relief in the early years at being free of his critical ear and eye. But time had worn away that illusion, and I still struggled to hold both his enormous gifts to us and his destructiveness comfortably in my heart.

"I feel closer to Daddy," Miriam said sweetly, as we got into the car. Yet the father she had embraced in this belated retrieval was still the stern judge who would find no mitigating circumstances to excuse her broken life.

THE RAIN HAD held off while we were at the hospital and the cemetery. But by the time we finished our late breakfast and were on the road headed south, it was raining steadily. Miriam was driving again, carefully, easily, despite the rain, which she only rarely experiences in sunny California. She liked the feel of the little rented car, and driving highlighted her competence. After all, she had controlled her sorrow; and she hadn't even, despite the temptations of travel, gone off her diet.

We followed local roads in New Hampshire and part of Massachusetts, but when we reached Holyoke I wanted to increase our speed. Pulling to the side of the road, under the protection of an old chestnut tree, we both dashed around the front of the car to switch seats. Then we were on Interstate Highway 91 for the grueling last 150 miles back to New York.

As if the heavens had unfolded in an outpouring of anguish, sheets of dark rain rendered the windshield useless and blinded us with the spray of each passing car. Though our silence was now the comfort of a successful grieving, it also contained the sadness of moving ever farther from the grave we were unlikely to revisit in the foreseeable future. Miriam felt it too: she said, "Carol, four hours ago we were there," and then, "Carol, it seems so odd that we're going away from him now." At some point the previous night, she had stopped backing up on each phrase; she was no longer stuttering.

The windshield wipers hurried to and fro across the window and slapped each time against the bottom frame. I was getting tense from the effort to see through the downpour, and the wipers were making me dizzy. For the first time, I noticed that we had a radio and asked Miriam to poke around for something to listen to. Despite her refusal of music lessons, she has always listened to classical music: it is part of the dense, lonely melancholy of our European childhood home that we both have brought into our adult lives.

It was the Hartford FM station, from which issued a succession of beautiful offerings—a Rossini aria for soprano, a Beethoven cello sonata, a Bach or perhaps a Boccherini cantata. Hours of music as rich as bittersweet chocolate, satiating yet leaving that terrible hunger and regret. Capturing the pulse of our sorrow, they were all requiems. Through the windows that were momentarily swept clear, then again opaque with hard-driving rain, I kept track of the busy highway. Inside, with Miriam beside me, I found myself back in the devotional trance of our childhood living room, behind which the windshield wipers slapped the windowpane.

Notes

1. Harriet Pass Friedenrich, *Jewish Politics in Vienna, 1918–1938* (Bloomington & Indianapolis: Indiana University Press, 1991).
2. Israëlitische Kultusgemeinde Wien, *Der Wiener Stadttempel* (Wien, 1995).
3. Franz Wiesenhofer, *Gefangen unter Habsburgs Krone: K.u.K. Kriegsgefangenenlager in Erlauftal* (Purgstall: Franz Wiesenhofer, 1997).
4. Cited in George E. Berkeley, *Vienna and Its Jews: The Tragedy of Success, 1880s–1980s* (Cambridge, MA: ABT Books, 1988), 158.
5. The story of Bernfeld's organizing is told in Willi Hoffer and Siegfried Bernfeld, "'Jerubbal': An Episode in the Jewish Youth Movement," (New York: Leo Baeck Institute, 1965), 10:55–56; and Philip Utley, "Siegfried Bernfeld's Jewish Order of Youth, 1914–1922" (New York: Leo Baeck Institute, 1979), 24:319–69, 1979.
6. Siegfried Bernfeld, *Kinderheim Baumgarten: Bericht über einen ernsthafen Versuch mit neuer Erziehung* (Berlin: Jüdischer Verlag, 1921).
7. See Paul Roazen, *Freud and His Followers* (New York: Knopf, 1975), 451; E. Adam, "Siegfried Bernfeld und die Reformpädagogik," in K. Fallend and J. Reichmayr, eds., *Siegfried Bernfeld oder Die Grenzen der Psychoanalyses* (Frankfurt am Main: Stroemfeld/Nexus, 1992), 91–95.
8. Anna Freud, "Introduction to Psychoanalysis: Lectures for Child Analysts and Teachers, 1922–1935," in *The Writings of Anna Freud* (New York: International Universities Press, 1974), 1:128.
9. Sheldon Gardner and Gwendolyn Stevens, *Red Vienna and the Golden Age of Psychology: 1918–1938* (New York: Praeger, 1992), 98ff.
10. August Aichhorn, *Verwahrloste Jugend* (Wien, Zurich: Internationaler

Psychoanalystischer Verlag, 1925). Published in English as *Wayward Youth* (New York: Viking, 1935, and Imago, 1951).

11. Schwartz, Lawrence H., M.D., "From Vienna to Seattle: Dr. Edith Buxbaum Remembers." An interview.(Seattle, WA: Seattle Institute for Psychoanalysis, 1990), 16.

12. This argument is made by Anson Rabinbach in *The Crisis of Austrian Socialism* (Chicago: University of Chicago, 1983), 33.

13. Marie Jahoda, "The Migration of Psychoanalysis: Its Impact on American Psychology," in Donald Fleming and Bernard Bailyn, *The Intellectual Migration: Europe and America, 1930–1960* (Cambridge: Harvard University Press, 1969), 427.

14. Paul Bergman, "Neurotic Anxieties in Children and Their Prevention," *The Nervous Child*, 1946, 5:37–55.

15. Paul Bergman and Sibylle Escalona, "Unusual Sensitivities in Very Young Children," *The Psychoanalytic Study of the Child*, 1949, 3–4:333–52.

16. Paul Bergman, "The Objectivity of Criminological Science," in Kurt R. Eissler, ed., *Searchlights on Delinquency: New Psychoanalytic Studies* (Dedicated to Professor August Aichhorn, on the Occasion of his Seventieth Birthday.) (New York: International Universities Press, 1948).

17. The story of the Vienna Psychoanalytic Institute during the war is documented in Thomas Aichhorn (December 12, 1998). "1946 Wiedereröffnung der Wiener Psychoanalytischen Vereinigung," Vortrag Festtag, Wiener Psychoanalytiker Verein. In addition, material is from "August Aichhorn: 1878–1949, Friend of the Wayward Youth," in Franz Alexander, Samuel Eisenstein, and Martin Grotjahn, eds., *Psychoanalytic Pioneers* (New York: Basic Books, 1966), 348–59; and "August Aichhorn, 1878–1949," in Else Mühlleitner, *Biographisches Lexikon der Psychoanalyse* (Tübingen: Edition Diskord, 1992), 20–23.

18. Paul Bergman, "Neurotic Anxieties in Children and Their Prevention," *The Nervous Child*, 1946, 5:37–55.

19. Paul Bergman, "Music in the Thinking of Great Philosophers." *Music Therapy*, 1952, 4–44.